around San diego
WITH KIDS

CREDITS
Writer: Cynthia Cuadra Winters

Series Editors: Karen Cure, Andrea Lehman
Editor: Paul Eisenberg
Editorial Production: Kristin Milavec
Production/Manufacturing: Robert B. Shields

Design: Fabrizio La Rocca, *creative director;*
Tigist Getachew, *art director*
Illustration and Series Design: Rico Lins,
Keren Ora Admoni/Rico Lins Studio

ABOUT THE WRITER

Cynthia Cuadra Winters grew up in San Diego and has lived there for more than 25 years. She is the mother of three and aunt to 22 (and counting). She writes about family-related subjects for *San Diego Family Magazine* and has written about jewelry and other arts for *Lapidary Journal and Ornament.*

Fodor's Around San Diego with Kids

First Edition
ISBN 1-4000-1165-5
ISSN 1541-3209

IMPORTANT TIP

Although all prices, opening times, and other details in this book are based on information supplied to us at press time, changes occur all the time in the travel world, and Fodor's cannot accept responsibility for facts that become outdated or for inadvertent errors or omissions. So always confirm information when it matters, especially if you're making a detour to visit a specific place.

SPECIAL SALES

Fodor's Travel Publications are available at special discounts for bulk purchases for sales promotions or premiums. Special editions, including personalized covers, excerpts of existing guides, and corporate imprints, can be created in large quantities for special needs. For more information, contact your local bookseller or Special Markets, Fodor's Travel Publications, 1745 Broadway, New York, New York 10019. Inquiries from Canada should be directed to your local Canadian bookseller or sent to Random House of Canada, Ltd., Marketing Dept., 2775 Matheson Boulevard East, Mississauga, Ontario L4W 4P7. Inquiries from the United Kingdom should be sent to Fodor's Travel Publications, 20 Vauxhall Bridge Road, London, England SW1V 2SA.

PRINTED IN THE UNITED STATES OF AMERICA
10 9 8 7 6 5 4 3 2 1

AROUND San diego WITH KIDS

by Cynthia Cuadra Winters

Fodor's Travel Publications
New York • Toronto • London • Sydney • Auckland

www.fodors.com

COUNTDOWN TO GOOD TIMES!

GET READY, GET SET!

I grew up in San Diego. I've lived here for more than 25 years, and now my husband (also home-grown) and I are raising our three kids here, too. We've lived in other cities, some better suited to our cultural interests. But all roads have always led us back here, because no city surpasses San Diego as a place to be with kids. It's perpetually sunny and perpetually friendly. And above all, you don't have to work hard to find fun things to see and do.

Traveling with kids, ideally, includes a mix of blockbuster destinations and quieter, calmer, shorter pursuits. That's what I've tried to do in this book. Some of the obligatory biggies, such as the zoo and SeaWorld, may warrant a day or two, but many of the choices target kid-size attention spans—about an hour and a half to two hours of engaging activity. Along the way, I've tried to share a few tips from my family's many trips to these spots to spare you from those unpleasantries that can sour even the sunniest of Southern California days.

Above all, bear in mind that San Diego is large and sprawling. It's hard to even define the center of the city. For these purposes, I've listed distance information in this book as if traveling from downtown. The activities in the book span the county—like most native San Diegans, I think of the city as running west from the beach to the eastern reaches of the desert, and beginning north at Orange County and heading all the way south to Mexico's border. So when I say "around" San Diego with kids, I really mean it.

CONSIDER A CAR

When visiting San Diego you will want to rent a car. And if you do, know that California law requires that all children under age 6 and weighing less than 60 pounds ride in a car seat. If your 5½-year-old squawks at this, explain that the money you'd shell out for a traffic ticket would be better spent on souvenirs—this works for me. Most car rental agencies should have these guidelines available, along with car seats for rent.

Freeways are generally the fastest routes for travel around the county. Just try to stay off of them during rush hour. Your main thoroughfares will be I–5 (north and south near the coast), I–805 (north and south inland), I–15 (north and south even farther inland), I–8 (running east and west from the beach area), and I–94 (beginning in the west at downtown San Diego and running east). Rush hour tends to be worst on 5 and 15 south, 8 west, and 805 north in the mornings, and in the reverse in the evenings. Usually, you can scoot around town pretty freely between 9 and 4 and again after 6:30.

For nondrivers, public transportation is improving in San Diego, especially with the trolley system, which will get you to at least a third of the sights in this book. You should also be able to negotiate the clusters of attractions in Downtown, Old Town, and especially Balboa Park (given ample coverage in these pages) without a vehicle. For general information on public transportation, call 800/COMMUTE or check out the Online Transit Information System at www.sdcommute.com.

DISCOUNTS AND DEALS

The San Diego Convention and Visitors Bureau (619/236–1212) is a great resource for current information on activities throughout town, and often has special discounts and coupons for attractions, too.

If you plan to visit a number of the museums in Balboa Park, which I encourage, buy a Passport to Balboa Park, available at the park's visitor office and many of the museums. The booklet grants admission to 13 of the park's museums for a reduced price (plus it can be used over a number of days) and includes deluxe admission to the zoo. There is also a special 3-for-1 Pass that's good for unlimited admission to the zoo, SeaWorld, and Wild Animal Park for five consecutive days. A two-park ticket, available from either the zoo or Wild Animal Park, will get you into both places. During October, zoo admission is free for kids, but this isn't a well-kept secret, so be prepared for crowds. Both SeaWorld and Legoland also offer multiday tickets that may end up saving you some money.

LOCAL EATS, LOCAL SPEAK

If you use a car, take advantage of drive-throughs, especially local Mexican places throughout town (of course, you can walk up to them, too). They go by many names—Alberto's, Roberto's, Adalberto's, Hilberto's—basically, anything ending in "–berto's." Some are local chains and some are independents, but they are generally all pretty good, plus cheaper and more authentic than the Mexican places you'd find in the beach areas, shopping centers, and other touristy places. Most of these spots have similar menus, but if you're not sure what your kids will like, try a cheese quesadilla (melted cheese in a flour tortilla), chips and guacamole, or rolled tacos with guacamole. Always sample the salsa before offering it to your little ones, as it will be spicy more often than not.

We wouldn't want you to struggle with some of our local parlance, so here's a little cheat sheet for some commonly mispronounced place names throughout San Diego County: Encinitas (En-sin-eet-as), El Cajon (El Ka-hone), La Jolla (La

Hoi-ya), Escondido (Es-con-deed-o), Otay Mesa (O-tie May-sa), Poway (Pow-way), San Ysidro (San Yi-see-droe). And please remember that the city of Tijuana, right across the border in Mexico, is not pronounced "Tee-a-wuana," but rather, "Tee-wuana" (even locals make this mistake).

FINAL THOUGHTS

San Diego has some great events that occur only once a year, but if you're in town during these times, check them out. You'll find listings in our local paper, the *San Diego Union Tribune*, or in these free publications: *San Diego Family Magazine* and the *Reader* (readily available throughout the county). Particularly noteworthy: June/July: San Diego County Fair in Del Mar; July or August (scheduled weekend varies annually): Comic-Con International at the Convention Center Downtown; September (usually first weekend after Labor Day): Street Scene, the largest outdoor music festival in California (three days, more than 90 bands on at least nine stages); and December Nights in Balboa Park (usually first weekend), a special holiday celebration for the community. And although a trip to Mexico is not listed in this book, don't miss the chance to visit Tijuana, Tecate Rosarita Beach, or Ensenada (or even farther south).

Most of San Diego is pretty safe, but use the same precautions you would use in any major city or its environs. Be sure to pack a stroller for kids 4 and younger; major attractions and some hotels rent them, but it pays to have one on hand. Once you get to where you're going, especially around Balboa Park and many outdoor attractions, there's more walking than most toddlers will want to do in one day.

Because San Diego is so kid friendly, there truly could be another 60 listings here. But the mix of standards and local favorites in these pages are ones my family and friends have returned to over and over again. All are fun and enriching, and, above all, are tried and true kid-pleasers. I hope you agree, and that you'll share your experiences at these sights with us. Or, make a case for a place that should be in the book next time. E-mail us at editors@fodors.com (specify Around San Diego with Kids on the subject line), or write to us at Around San Diego with Kids, Fodor's Travel Publications, 1745 Broadway, New York, New York 10019. In the meantime, see you around town!

—Cynthia Cuadra Winters

ARCO U.S. OLYMPIC TRAINING CENTER

60

Do you dream of taking the kids to the Olympic Games someday? In the meantime, you can bring them here to see where some of America's best athletes do their training. One of only three official training centers in the United States (the others are in New York and Colorado), this one, built in 1995, is the newest and biggest, set on 150 acres nestled into natural countryside next to a lake. It is devoted to summer sports such as softball, track and field, canoeing/kayaking, cycling, rowing, soccer, archery, and field hockey.

To see most of the grounds, take the guided walking tour—it's about 2 mi and lasts an hour (good for school-age kids). Your little sluggers will get to see the fields where the two-time gold medal–winning U.S. Women's Softball Team practices. You'll also see the 400-meter track, training areas for field events, the cycling tunnel and trails, various playing fields, and the largest permanent archery field in North America. From the Olympic Path

KEEP IN MIND If you visit the center in the morning or afternoon, you will better your chances of seeing some athletes practicing (they go in at lunchtime). You can increase your odds by doing what the locals do—call ahead to find out the training schedules. The public is usually welcome to watch as long as they don't disturb the athletes—this works best with kids 9 and older. Be forewarned that practices can be changed or canceled at the last minute.

 2800 Olympic Pkwy.,
Chula Vista

 Free

 Visitor Center M–Sa 10–5,
Su 11–5; tours hourly M–F 10–3,
Sa 9–4, Su 11–3

 619/482–6222

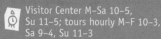 6 and up

you walk along, there is a good view of Lower Otay Lake, where the athletes take their boats out for canoeing, kayaking, and rowing. Not all of the summer sports are practiced here (no gymnastics or swimming), but there are plans to add water polo and synchronized swimming.

If the tour seems too much for younger kids, you can explore on your own if you stay on the designated path. You'll begin and end your trip at the Copley Visitor's Center. Inside is a theater with a short introductory film, a miniature scale model of the center, rest rooms, water fountains, and a shop. Before you leave, check out the burning Olympic flame that rises high above the plaza: it was first lit by the Olympic torch as it passed through here on its way to the Atlanta Summer Games in 1996.

EATS FOR KIDS
Stop for pizza or pasta on the way out to the center at nearby **D'Lish** (2260 Otay Lakes Rd., 619/216–3900). Or, try the Mexican food at **Alejandro's** (2220 Otay Lakes Rd., 619/216–8812). Vending machines are all you'll find at the training center.

HEY, KIDS! About 4,000 athletes come here every year to practice, but it's also a lot like summer camp: they live in dorms, hang out with other athletes, and play outside all day. As many as 175 stay here at a time, with three or four to a room, and they all eat together in a cafeteria. It's so much fun, even some winter sports athletes (like bobsledders) and athletes from other countries come here for special training.

BALBOA PARK

Let's say you were pressured to pick just two destinations while in San Diego. You'd likely pick a beach—and the other one? Choose Balboa Park. But what about the world-famous San Diego Zoo, you say? Don't worry, it's here, along with 15 museums and more than 80 other cultural attractions.

The zoo warrants a full-day trip of its own (*see #14*), so save another day (or two) for Balboa Park. The 1,200-acre urban park is just up the hill from downtown San Diego. If you have only a few hours to spend here, take a walk down the central Prado area and hit a museum or two. The Natural History Museum (*see #16*) and the Reuben H. Fleet Science Center (*see #26*) are good for all ages. If you have more time, toddlers and preschoolers might enjoy the Marie Hitchcock Puppet Theatre (*see #34*); then stop by the Japanese

GETTING THERE The Balboa Park Free Tram offers transportation within the park; pick it up at any of the marked spots. It runs daily from 8:30 to 6. It also picks up from the Inspiration Point Parking lot on the east side of Park Boulevard near President's Way.

KEEP IN MIND Pick up a Passport to Balboa Park (it will get you into 13 of the parks attractions for $30, and it's good for a week). The museums offer free admission on rotating Tuesdays throughout the month, so check out the schedule while you're here (this usually applies to regular exhibitions, not special presentations). For example, the Reuben H. Fleet Science Center, San Diego Natural History Museum, and San Diego Model Railroad Museum have free admission on the first Tuesday of each month.

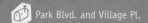 Park Blvd. and Village Pl.

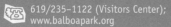 619/235-1122 (Visitors Center);
www.balboapark.org

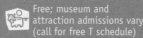 Free; museum and
attraction admissions vary
(call for free T schedule)

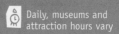 Daily, museums and
attraction hours vary

 All ages

Friendship Garden to feed the Koi fish, pop into the Model Railroad Museum (*see #19*), and finish up with rides on a real mini-train and carousel (*see #58*) near the zoo entrance.

Head to the south end of the park with elementary school–age kids, who'll enjoy the sports at the Hall of Champions (*see #22*) and the planes and cars at the aerospace and automotive museums (*see #24*). Back at the Prado, stop by Mingei International Museum to see its colorful and exotic world folk art. Also try to catch the all-kid cast at a Junior Theatre performance (*see #21*). Teens and kids with more sophisticated tastes can take in the collections at the Museum of Art (*see #18*) and the Museum of Photographic Arts, and maybe even a Shakespearean play at the Old Globe Theatre complex. In contrast, they'll also relish the gross-out factor of seeing some real, and rather grisly, mummies at the Museum of Man (*see #17*).

BALBOA PARK MINI-TRAIN AND CAROUSEL

R are are amusement areas made just for the tiniest tots, but this little quartet of rides on the edge of Balboa Park is geared for the 5-and-under set. None of the rides are scary, and, as an extra special treat for you and your kids, neither are the lines.

The rides sit on an island of grass just outside the entrance to the San Diego Zoo's parking lot. The carousel, built in 1910 in New York, has been enjoyed in Balboa Park since 1922, and nearly all of its animals are originals. They are hand-carved and brightly painted, with a menagerie of steeds to choose from. The interior murals are hand-painted, and this merry-go-round has one of the few brass ring games left in the world: the lucky rider who can grasp the ring on the way around gets a free ride. The rousing military band music is the same that has played here for more than 80 years, and the ride is a blessed five minutes long.

KEEP IN MIND   A visit to these little rides is the perfect way to end a trip to Balboa Park's other destinations, or it can warrant a trip of its own. The closest place to park near the rides is in the zoo's parking lot, which is free. If you want to make this a full-morning outing, bring along a picnic to enjoy after the rides and let the kids run around on the grass.

 Zoo Place in Balboa Park

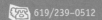 619/239-0512

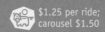 $1.25 per ride; carousel $1.50

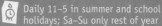 Daily 11–5 in summer and school holidays; Sa–Su only rest of year

 5 and under

Next, the little ones can fly through the air (though comfortably low to the ground) in an airplane or on the back of a colorful butterfly. These two rides are only for kids under 5, so they can smugly beam at their siblings as they finally get to do something that the older ones can't.

After this you can wait at the official-looking depot to board the miniature train ride. The one-fifth-scale-size choo-choo goes on a ½-mi ride through a 4-acre section of Balboa Park. The rare model G-16 is one of only 50 left, and it has been running here since 1948. And you won't miss the fun this time, because you can hop aboard, too.

EATS FOR KIDS

There are food carts with hot dogs and snacks near the museums at the park. Or, head to the **Village Grill** in the park (corner of Village Pl. and Old Globe Way) for burgers and fries that you can enjoy at outdoor tables.

HEY, KIDS! The miniature train ride is only one-fifth the size of a real train, but if you want to see some even smaller ones, head over to the San Diego Model Railroad Museum (see #19) in nearby Balboa Park. There are plenty of cool little trains here, and even niftier are the little scenarios they chug through, stocked with miniature people, animals, houses, and trees.

BASIC BROWN BEAR FACTORY

57

If you have crafty kids (the good kind), here's a place where they can create something substantial—and then hug it afterward. They'll pick from several bears, choose a color, and work the machine that stuffs the bear. They'll also be able to outfit and accessorize it, so essentially, any kid who comes here gets a chance to be a toy designer (it will look great on their resumes later).

This concept grew out of factory tours given by the company in their original San Francisco factory. The experience was so popular that "mini-factories" like this one in Old Town were born. You can just settle for watching other customers construct the bears, but if you're making this trip, bite the bullet and let the kids make one. There are many sizes and styles,

EATS FOR KIDS **Fred's Mexican Café** (2470 San Diego Ave., 619/858-8266) has both Mexican and American dishes, including cheeseburgers. For Mexican food with shrimp and other fish, try **Amigos Seafood** (2470 San Diego Ave., 619/260-3624).

HEY, KIDS! You may have heard that teddy bears were named after President Theodore (Teddy) Roosevelt, but do you know why? It all came about from a hunting trip where instead of shooting a captured bear, he decided to let it go free. That lucky bear (reportedly a 235-pound black bear) became known as Teddy's Bear after a popular cartoon about the incident appeared in the newspaper. As the story was repeated, it changed some and the giant bear started to be described as a little cub instead. Not long after that, teddy bears more or less as we know them went into production.

 2375 San Diego Ave.

 Free; bear prices vary

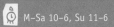 M–Sa 10–6, Su 11–6

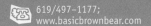 619/497–1177;
www.basicbrownbear.com

 3 and up

beginning at $12 and ascending to as much as $150 (and even higher for custom designs). Fortunately, there are several good ones to choose from in the under-$20 range.

After kids choose their bear and its "skin," they get to stuff it, using a colorful machine resembling an arcade game. There are about 30 possible bears—but if these mammals aren't your kids' thing, they can craft a rabbit, moose, lamb, or dragon. About 40 or so outfits and accessories—princess, pilot, cowboy, ballerina, and other popular vocations—can be bought at an additional charge, and here's where costs add up. It might be better to save the accessories for future occasions, after you know the bear is going to endure as a plaything in your house; you can purchase them at the company's other locations or from its Web site.

KEEP IN MIND For more creative fun, take the kids a couple of blocks northwest to 2802 Juan Street. Here you'll find unusual and intriguing beads from all over the world at Lost Cities (619/692–1114) and The Shepherdess (619/297–4110). They each also offer classes in jewelry-making techniques. Between them in the same complex is Stampaholics (619/295–3712), a shop filled with hundreds of rubber stamps, brass stencils, inks, and papers so kids can make their own stationery, cards, or other paper art pieces.

BAZAAR DEL MUNDO

This place not only looks like fun, but also feels like walking into a celebration any day of the week. Dazzling the senses are bursts of festively colored flowers, a bubbling fountain, lively music, the smell of good food, and much more. Bazaar del Mundo is the cultural heir of San Diego's rich Mexican, South American, and Native American roots, and on top of that, it's right inside San Diego's historic Old Town, the most-visited state park in California.

This may be one of the few tourist spots that is visited equally by tourists and locals. For the last 30 years, San Diegans have loved coming here for the year-round cultural activities, weekly free folkloric entertainment, 16 boutiques, and 5 restaurants. Kids love walking around the charming courtyard, where free music and dance performances—such as marimba bands, traditional Hispanic folk dancing, flamenco, and Peruvian music—are offered daily (performance times vary throughout the day between 10 and 5). Walk over to the Casa De Pico Restaurant on the eastern end of the courtyard and see how fresh tortillas are made (3–8 W–Su) or see demonstrations of Mexican paper flower making at Artes de Mexico (10–5 Th–Su).

EATS FOR KIDS Of course, most of the restaurants here offer Mexican fare. **Casa de Pico** (619/296–3267) gets the most attention, as it's in the courtyard, but it can get crowded and you can do well at any of the other restaurants here. **Rancho el Nopal** (619/295–0584) has strolling musicians and a children's menu. If the kids would rather have spaghetti than a burrito, try **Lino's** (619/299–7124). For dessert or a snack, take the kids into **La Panderia** on the courtyard, where they can walk out with a warm *churro*, a Mexican pastry covered with sugar and cinnamon.

 2754 Calhoun St.

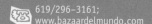 619/296-3161;
www.bazaardelmundo.com

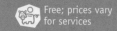 Free; prices vary
for services

 Daily 10–9

 All ages

Seasonal artist demonstrations, special performances, folk art exhibits, and international vendors underscore the region's rich cultural heritage, including the Santa Fe Market (March), Cinco de Mayo Celebration (May), Mercado del Sol (June), an 1800s Fourth of July celebration, Latin American Festival (August), Mexican Independence Day (September), Dia de los Muertos (October 26–November 2), and the Festival of Lights (November/December).

Exit the southern end of the bazaar (near the carriage) for easy walking access to the rest of Old Town (*see #30*), where you can see the first European settlement in all of California. Then head southeast to the state's first brick building, the Thomas Whaley House Museum (*see #6*)—it's also an official haunted house!

KEEP IN MIND
The bazaar is in an old building with narrow doorways, so the shops here are not all stroller friendly, but bring it along; you can always park it outside, and you will want it when you explore the rest of Old Town State Park.

HEY, KIDS! With Mexico just a few miles south of here, it's a good idea to be able to speak a little Spanish when visiting San Diego. For instance, *hola* means hello, and *por favor* means please. Here are some other phrases you may find handy around grown-ups: *Tengo hambre!* means I'm hungry! *Tengo sed!* means I'm thirsty! And *Mi gustaria ir al parque de atracciones!* means I would like to go to the amusement park! Remember to add *por favor* to these phrases, and don't forget to say, *Muchas gracias!* (Thank you very much!).

BELMONT PARK

J ust like chocolate and peanut butter, an amusement park and a beach is a happy marriage; Belmont Park is just steps from Mission Beach.

The park's crown jewel is the 1925 wooden roller coaster, the Giant Dipper, its gracefully looping tracks rising above the park's other rides, shops, and arcade. During the minute-and-45-second ride you'll travel 2,600 ft of track at up to 45 mph; the highest drop is from 75 ft up. After 50 years of popular use, the Dipper began to fall apart and was closed in 1976. But the community worked to save it, and it reopened, fully restored, in 1990.

The coaster is mainly for the older kids (must be 50 inches tall to ride), but other rides cater to the littler ones (like gentle carnival-type vehicle rides and the Liberty Carousel

EATS FOR KIDS Pirate's Cove on the southeastern corner of Belmont Park has pizza and other kid-friendly fare. There are also food kiosks throughout the park with hot dogs, pizza, burgers, churros (Mexican sugar-and-cinnamon-covered pastry), drinks, ice cream, and candy.

KEEP IN MIND Belmont Park charges $2–$4 for each ride. They do have specially priced ticket packages, but be sure to check out the rides before you buy; some have height restrictions, so your younger children won't be able to ride all of them. The park usually has Family Fun Nights with reduced prices during the summer.

 3190 Mission Blvd.

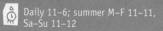 $4 Giant Dipper, $2-$4 other rides, $6.50 Pirate's Cove 12 and under (adult free with child)

 Daily 11–6; summer M–F 11–11, Sa–Su 11–12

 858/488-1549; www.giantdipper.com

1 and up

with murals depicting San Diego's history). Kids elementary school age and under will also like the indoor Pirate's Cove, with a 7,000-sq-ft climbing structure with slides, ladders, and a smaller area for toddlers to play in. There's also a small arcade and eatery within.

Older kids 9 and up would probably rather hang out outside, ride the Giant Dipper, Vertical Plunge, or Tilt-A-Whirl, and visit the big arcade. These attractions will also appeal to teens, but they may prefer to spend most of their time on the beach. You can take them across the street and one block north to Hamel's Action Sports (704 Ventura Pl., 858/488-5050), where you can rent beach and boardwalk equipment, including Boogie Boards, Rollerblades, skateboards, and bikes. Of course, you can just head west to the beach for a free swim, or go east across Mission Boulevard to Ventura Cove at Mission Bay Park (*see #33*), where the kids can run and play for free.

HEY, KIDS! The very first roller coasters were actually very large slides—and they were made of ice! Back in the 16th century, Russians built ice slides. The understructure was made of wood with a thick layer of ice on the surface. The tallest ones got to be about 80 ft tall, and the riders would go down on sleds. Riders didn't generally have to wait in long lines, but they did have to climb up ladderlike steps every time they wanted to ride.

BIRCH AQUARIUM AT SCRIPPS

Unlike your garden-variety theme-park type of aquarium, this one has some serious brain power behind it. This is the public education arm of the Scripps Institute of Oceanography at University of California, San Diego, which does some of the world's most cutting-edge research on the ocean and marine life. So you know that any information the kids pick up here comes straight from the seahorse's mouth.

The luminescent glow from the aquariums draws you into the dark and mysterious-looking Hall of Fishes, where you'll discover 46 tanks with fish, corals, and invertebrates from the West Coast, Mexico's Sea of Cortez, and tropical seas. There are special exhibits devoted to sharks (always a favorite), seahorses, and hypnotically beautiful jellyfish. Kids also get a chance to see what San Diego looks like underwater when peering into the 70,000-gallon kelp forest tank that mirrors the environment found here just off the coast.

KEEP IN MIND Be sure to check whether any of the aquarium's seasonal exhibits will be held during the time of your visit. Look for Shark Discovery Days in summer, Whale-fest in winter, and the Haunted Aquarium at Halloween. You can also call ahead to reserve space for special programs; there are several offered each quarter, such as snorkeling classes, whale-watching cruises, pier walks, grunion sightings, and lectures and workshops designed for kids. The whole family can "sleep with the fishes" in their overnight programs, where you get to spend the night in the aquarium.

2300 Expedition Way, La Jolla

858/534–FISH;
www.aquarium.ucsd.edu

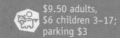
$9.50 adults,
$6 children 3–17;
parking $3

Daily 9–5 (except major holidays)

2 and up

It's quite a contrast to then enter the brightly lit Hall of Oceanography that has the largest exhibit on this science in the country. Little kids love prodding and poking all the levers and buttons on the interactive displays, which help illustrate some of the research done down the hill at Scripps Institute. Be sure to take a look at the "supermarket" exhibit that illustrates how sea life is vital to the products we use every day.

Another hands-on favorite is the Outdoor Plaza with its demonstration tide pool—kids can stick their hands in and get a personal look at some examples of the local sea life. When you're finished here, you can always take them down the hill to La Jolla Shores Beach (*see #40*), where they can continue their studies with a little underwater exploration of their own.

EATS FOR KIDS
There is a food stand here with sandwiches and snacks. Or head up the hill 1½ mi near the U.C.S.D. campus, where serviceable fare includes the **California Pizza Kitchen** (3363 Nobel Dr., 858/457–4222) and **Samson's Deli** (8861 Villa La Jolla Dr., 858/455–1461).

HEY, KIDS! Are sea horses really tiny horses that swim? Nope, they just look like horses because of their long, tubular mouths. And their tails are prehensile just like a monkey's. But they are actually fish—despite their oddities. Did you know that the male sea horses give birth to the babies? Drop by the sea horse nursery here to get a look at the tiny newborns. Then you can check out their relatives, the sea dragons, in tank 33, resembling part sea horse, part leafy green plant.

CABRILLO NATIONAL MONUMENT

There's a lot happening on this tiny point of land surrounded on three sides by water. Thousands of gray whales swing by here annually, and rare coastal sage and chaparral ecology abound. There are historical structures to see, and the point has the only federally protected tide pools in Southern California. Not incidentally, this is also where Juan Rodriguez Cabrillo "discovered" the West Coast of this new world in the 16th century.

So, what should you check out first? There are two distinct areas to visit here. Start with the historical stuff near the visitor center, because once kids get a load of the tide pools you'll never get them back here. From the visitor center, it's an easy walk over to see the statue of Cabrillo that looks out toward the ocean at the spot where his expedition first encountered this coastline. Then walk over to the Old Point Loma Lighthouse, where you

EATS FOR KIDS You can picnic at the point, but there isn't any food sold here. Stop on the way at **Point Loma Seafoods** (2805 Emerson St., 619/223–1109) for delicious chowders and sandwiches, or cruise by **Adalberto's** (1868 Rosecrans St., 619/224–4440) for some take-out Mexican food.

HEY, KIDS! Juan Rodriguez Cabrillo wasn't looking for this place when he showed up in 1542. He was trying to find a route to Asia, to get valuable spices and silk for trade, but along the way, he discovered this piece of land that is now Point Loma. He and his crew never made it to Asia—and poor Cabrillo died from an accident just a few months after his discovery. But the rest of his expedition was able to return to Mexico (then called New Spain) with another kind of treasure—a map of the coastline that would someday become California.

 1800 Cabrillo Memorial Dr.

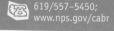 619/557-5450;
www.nps.gov/cabr

 $5 per car, $3
pedestrians and bicycles,
ages 16 and under free

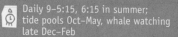 Daily 9–5:15, 6:15 in summer;
tide pools Oct–May, whale watching
late Dec–Feb

 2 and up

can go inside to see period furnishings such as china, kerosene lamps, and decorative art that belonged to the last keeper, Robert Israel, and his family, who lived here until 1891. Bring along binoculars if you're here late December through February so you can check the horizon for signs of migrating whales (hint: look for breathing spouts and flapping tails). You can also hike the 2-mi Bayside Trail that loops through the native landscape and passes by the military structures used here as defense points during both world wars.

You'll need to get back in the car and drive south to the tide pools. Here, you'll get to explore the shallow ocean pools that are revealed in the rocks only at low tide. The whole family will be captivated by the amazing creatures you'll get to see and touch, including shore crabs, bat stars (a type of sea star), sea anemones, limpets, and small octopuses.

KEEP IN MIND The tide pools are not to be missed, so try to come in season, October–May. You must also come during a minus tide (check the newspaper). Even then you must watch for high surf waves because they can flow across the tide pools unexpectedly. The rocks are very slippery, so be sure everyone wears sneakers or pool shoes (and bring towels, as feet and hands—and maybe more—will get wet). The kids can touch the creatures in the tide pools, as long as they don't harm them or take anything (not even seashells—they're protected here!).

CAJON SPEEDWAY

Even if your kids were never that into revving Hot Wheels on every surface in your house, they might still be impressed by the life-size versions that hug the track here at speeds of up to 160 mph. On Saturday nights, close to 3,000 fans pack the stands to see NASCAR weekly racing series competitors drive what's been described as "the fastest ⅜-mi paved oval on the west coast."

They've been racing here in El Cajon—about 15 mi east of San Diego—since 1961, on one of only 100 short tracks in the country. NASCAR (National Association for Stock Car Auto Racing) is fast becoming one of the most popular spectator sports in the country, but if this happens to be your first trip to the track, here's a primer: stock cars are basically American-made passenger cars (at the core, like any Fords or Chryslers on the road), but their bodies or engines have been modified to different degrees to make them faster. There are variations on the stock types, such as sprints and midgets (smaller and faster) and the odd-looking "train," composed of three cars stuck together to make one long vehicle.

KEEP IN MIND When you come to the races, try to sit as high up in the grandstand as possible. Although there are special crash walls and safety structures constructed to protect spectators, it's always best to elevate your brood in case of an accident to avoid potential flying debris. For sensitive ears, it's also a good idea to bring along a set of earplugs for everyone, as the roar of engines (plus the cheers of the crowd) can reach pretty high decibel levels.

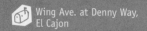 Wing Ave. at Denny Way, El Cajon

 $10 ages 13 and up, $3 children 6–12; parking $1

 Qualifying starts at 5:15; races begin 6:45 Mar–Oct

 619/448-8900; www.cajonsspeedway.com

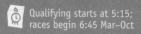 3 and up

Kids will enjoy the sound of the engines, the roar of the crowd, and the spectacle of the colorful cars zipping by, but let's face it, most of all they'll like the crashes. Luckily, NASCAR has very specific safety regulations for the cars to help prevent serious injuries to the drivers.

Real race fanatics can come out to the track earlier in the day and watch the practices for free (usually from 10 to 4). During the evening races, they can also tune in to radio frequencies to hear the conversations between the drivers and their crew (but be warned—sometimes the language they'll overhear might get a little "spirited").

EATS FOR KIDS
Concessions here sell hot dogs, burgers, pizza, and snacks. You can bring in food, but you'll have to eat in the bleachers. Stop for dinner at **Grandstand Pizza** (1571 N. Magnolia, 619/258–6488) or seafood specialties at **La Casita Taco Shop** (1503 N. Magnolia, 619/444–8228).

HEY, KIDS! They use flags at the races to communicate with the drivers who are traveling around the track too fast to stop and talk. The colors on each flag have different meanings: Green = start the race; red = stop!; yellow = caution; half red and half yellow = race needs to be restarted; black with white stripe = your car has a mechanical problem, so pull over to the pit for service; black = pull over to the pit immediately! (sometimes indicates a penalty); white = only one lap left to go; black and white checkered = the race is over!

CALIFORNIA CENTER FOR THE ARTS

I f by "performing arts," your kids think you're referring to an earnest school musical or a fire-juggling street clown (not that there's anything wrong with these), then the city of Escondido has thoughtfully created a venue that might broaden their exposure.

Littler kids in particular—say, ages 3 through 7—might enjoy the Mervyn's Theater for Family shows on Sunday afternoons, with a focus on animal folktales and fairy tales (performances are at 2 PM). Older and perhaps already more discerning patrons of the arts can sample jazz, blues, light opera, comedy, or Native American storytelling, among other offerings. Some of these performances, blissfully, are also free. The Wells Fargo First Wednesdays program includes classical guitar and Mozart concerts. Unless otherwise noted, these shows are in the Center Theater at 4 PM on the first Wednesday of the month; call for details.

KEEP IN MIND If the kids can't get enough art, they can see plenty more at "2nd Saturday Escondido." A monthly program sponsored by Escondido Arts Partnership (760/480–4101), it's a free, self-guided art walk through local galleries, studios, theaters, and antique dealers.

EATS FOR KIDS For a real treat, stop at **Major Market** (1855 S. Center City Pkwy., Escondido, 760/741–8773). It looks like a mild-mannered grocery store on the outside, but inside there are amazing, freshly prepared foods to eat there or take out, like gourmet deli items, soups, hot entrees, and scrumptious bakery items. Just across from the center is the **Arista Café & Bistro** (427 N. Escondido Blvd., 760/745–5461) for sandwiches and desserts. Or, try **Ma Cuch's Italian Restaurant** (391 N. Escondido Blvd., 760/480–6313) for pasta and pizza, or **Mariachi's Mexican Food** (501 N. Escondido Blvd., 760/740–8581) for seafood specialties.

340 N. Escondido Blvd.,
Escondido

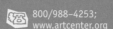800/988-4253;
www.artcenter.org

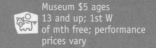Museum $5 ages
13 and up; 1st W
of mth free; performance
prices vary

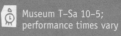Museum T–Sa 10–5;
performance times vary

3 and up

In addition to these child-oriented programs, the center offers a full slate of performances geared toward adults, but plenty of these are also family friendly, such as the annual "Nutcracker" ballet as well as other dance pieces. International, national, and local groups, and soloists come to the center to perform, too. The San Diego Symphony and contemporary musicians such as Keb' Mo' have given concerts, and the center also has comedic performances and special events, such as "Sing-Along Sound of Music" and shows by such A-list celebrities as Franklin the Turtle.

Venues for these performances include the center's 1,500-seat concert hall and 400-seat theater. If you're looking to fill your day before or after performances, the center's 12-acre campus also has a sculpture garden and a museum with three galleries focusing on 20th- and 21st-century art (museum admission is free on the first Wednesday of each month).

GETTING THERE It's a 30-mi drive up here from San Diego, but this is a good companion trip if you are making the trek to Escondido for the Wild Animal Park (*see #15*). Take I–15 north to Valley Parkway, make a right at the light, travel east five blocks to Escondido Boulevard, turn left, and continue about two and a half blocks; you'll see the center on the right. Continue on and turn right into the parking lot. Just be sure to stay off I–15 during rush hour.

CALIFORNIA WOLF CENTER

I t's hard to believe that wolves are an endangered species. There used to be millions of them roaming North America, but there are only about 4,500 left in the lower 48 United States. The treat for you and your family is that you'll get to meet some of them here. This center is one of the only places in California where you can see North American gray wolves. The work done here helps protect wolves through education, research, and captive breeding.

The Saturday program lasts about two hours and has a slide show program and guided visits with the wolves that live here. The first 30 minutes of the program might be too much for littler ones, but school-age kids like the slides, and they get to see paw prints, bones, and skulls from wolves and prey, and can pet a real wolf pelt.

Then the big moment arrives, when you get to go outside and "meet" the wolves. First is a visit with four socialized wolves. Raised by humans, they're still wild animals and not for

HEY, KIDS! How did wolves become an endangered species in the United States? When the settlers came west and began farming and ranching, they hunted and trapped wolves because they didn't want them to eat their livestock. But when the settlers moved in, they had scared away the wolves' natural prey! With nothing left to eat, the wolves started hunting the cows and sheep to survive. Wolves became protected by the Endangered Species Act in 1974.

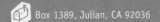 Box 1389, Julian, CA 92036

 619/234-WOLF, 760/765-0030;
www.californiawolfcenter.org

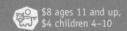 $8 ages 11 and up,
$4 children 4–10

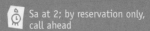 Sa at 2; by reservation only,
call ahead

 5 and up

petting, but you can see them up close in their enclosures. You may be surprised by their large size (average is 90 lb) and nearly white color (gray wolves actually come in many colors). You'll also learn that unless you are a caribou, moose, elk, deer, or bison, you don't have much to fear from wolves—they are more likely to run away from humans than attack them. Because they are shy with people, you'll be asked to crouch down low and speak quietly in front of their enclosure. The last part of the program gives you a rare sight, a captive pack of wild wolves (in California, the last known wild wolf was trapped in 1924). You'll get a good view of their enclosure from an observation area, and if you're really lucky, they might even give you a howl!

EATS FOR KIDS
Nearby Julian is filled with good eats. For barbecue and burgers, try **Rongranch Restaurant** (2722 Washington St., 760/765–2265). Or, stop by **Dudley's Bakery** on your way out of Julian (30218 Hwy. 78, Santa Ysabel, 800/220–3348) for their famous breads and bakery items.

GETTING THERE   You've got to have reservations to attend (they take only about 40 people each week), but they are easy to get. Just call ahead of time. The center is in the mountains, about 50 mi east of San Diego. On Highway 79 it's about 4 mi south of the town of Julian (a great companion trip for the day; *see #43*), and you'll be asked to turn off into the K. Q. Campground. You need to check in by 1:40 so you can be escorted to the center.

CHILDREN'S DISCOVERY MUSEUM

It's so refreshing to take the kids to a museum where you don't have to follow them around repeating, "Don't touch!" and "Ah-ah-ah!" and they—or you—aren't getting withering looks from the guards. Touching things here is not only permitted, but sincerely encouraged.

There's a lot to "discover" here at the Children's Discovery Museum of North County, especially about the arts, the environment, history, and science. Your kids can immediately get down to business making their own artwork at the Creative Corner (with a different type of project offered each week). Littler kids love to play "store" in the Kids' Marketplace, where nutritional education is introduced in packages and equipment that's been reduced to their size (and they will love the chance to turn the tables on you and tell you what you can and can't have on their shopping trip—so no whining). Your little knights can also defend the realm while dressed in their own set of armor and chain mail while

EATS FOR KIDS There are many kid-friendly places to eat in this area (sharing the street address of 300 Carlsbad Village Dr.): **Spirito's** (760/720–1132) for pizza and pasta, **Vinaka's** (760/720–7890) for sandwiches, soups, snacks, and ice cream, and **Neiman's** (760/729–4131) for seafood, steak, and Sunday brunch.

KEEP IN MIND If you can come to this area in early springtime, you'll be treated to a rare site: a hillside covered with tremendous bands of brilliantly colored flowers that resemble a rainbow (you can even see it from the freeway). Every year, the spectacular vision appears here at the Flower Fields of Carlsbad as thousands of Giant Tecolote Ranunculus flowers come into bloom. To visit the fields, take the Palomar Airport Road exit from I–5. They're open 9–5 early March through early May. Admission is $7 for ages 11 and up, $4 for children 3–10. For information, call 760/431–0352.

 300 Carlsbad Village Dr.,
#103, Carlsbad

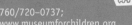 $4 ages 2 and up

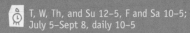 T, W, Th, and Su 12–5, F and Sa 10–5;
July 5–Sept 8, daily 10–5

760/720-0737;
www.museumforchildren.org

 1 and up

under the rule of the beautiful princess or majestic king (also in appropriate costumes) at the Castle Play area.

Older kids will enjoy the chance to make their own music in the World of Sound exhibit, where they can play a variety of instruments from different cultures. You can show them how the solar powers of the sun can be used to run a toy train and a plasma sphere (now if only their Gameboys could be solar powered, think how much you'd save on AA batteries).

The tiniest kids get their own place to discover shapes to play with and climb on in the Toddler Corner. And kids of all ages like the chance to climb aboard the Fishin' Boat, and go on a faux fishing trip off the coast of San Diego, using a magnetic fishing line to haul in some laminated pictures of the local fish found here.

HEY KIDS! Although many city names in San Diego County have Spanish language origins, Carlsbad is actually named after a 19th-century spa in Karlsbad, Bohemia. Not long after this part of the California coast was settled in the 1880s, mineral water was discovered here. At the time, it was believed that this water had special properties that could cure health problems. To promote the growing town, local landowners touted the mineral water as being similar to that found in the famous Karlsbad Spa, and the town here soon came to be known as Carlsbad.

CHULA VISTA NATURE CENTER

The Nature Center sits within the Sweetwater Marsh National Wildlife Refuge, which means that everything in this 316-acre area is protected: the birds, the sea creatures, the plants, in fact, the entire ecosystem. Kids can see rare and endangered species of birds and plants, along with another extraordinary sight: a part of the California coast in its natural state, devoid of the boardwalks and tourist attractions found along the coast north of here.

Inside the Nature Center's building are interactive exhibits that help explain the salt marsh environment to kids, allowing them to touch things, move parts, and peer into the mysteries found under the ground and water outside. Don't miss the 4,500-gallon shallow tank where they can reach in and "pet" the stingrays and leopard and horn sharks (don't worry, the sharks here aren't the limb-snacking kind). Then take them outdoors to see the burrowing owls, egrets, herons, and other shorebirds kept in enclosures.

GETTING THERE One way the Wildlife Refuge protects itself is by limiting the number of cars that can come in, so instead of driving directly to the Nature Center, they shuttle visitors in from the parking lot. You'll find it just west of the Bayfront/E Street exit off I–5 in Chula Vista (about 7 mi south of downtown San Diego). The shuttle comes by every 25 minutes beginning at 10 AM. You can also take the San Diego Trolley to the nearby E Street Station, where the shuttle stops to pick up visitors to the Nature Center.

 1000 Gunpowder Point Dr., Chula Vista

 619/409-5900; ChulaVistaNatureCenter.org

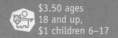 $3.50 ages 18 and up, $1 children 6–17

 June–Aug, T–Su 10–5

 2 and up

Your kids should get a kick out of climbing to the top of the two bird-watching platforms to get their own bird's-eye view of the surrounding marsh. Most kids seem to enjoy the easy hikes through the marsh toward the ocean. Along the paths, the older ones can use their newly acquired knowledge from the Nature Center to scout out some of the native flora and fauna. There are about 215 species of birds here to watch for (if you forget your binoculars, you can rent some from the bookstore). You'll also see the world's only exhibit of light-footed clapper rails, the most endangered waterbird in California—there are only about 350 of them left in the state.

EATS FOR KIDS
Aunt Emma's Pancake Restaurant (700 E St., 619/427-2722) has good old-fashioned breakfasts and many hearty lunch choices, too. Your picky ones will enjoy grazing the lunch buffet (with desserts) at **Royal China Palace II** (625 E St., 619/691-1678).

HEY, KIDS! The water in Sweetwater Marsh is actually quite salty. A marsh is land that is almost always covered with water, so it remains wet and fairly soft; this marsh is covered with salty seawater. It's a great place to grow worms, snails, clams, and other creatures that migrating birds dine on. It's critical to protect these types of environments because at least 75% of California's wetlands have been destroyed by development and waste dumping by humans.

CORONADO

There are two fun ways to get to Coronado Island—by boat or by bridge. The ride on the San Diego–Coronado Bay Ferry is a pleasant 15-minute trip across the water to the Ferry Market Plaza, which has shops and restaurants (*see #23*). If you go by car, you can cross the graceful Coronado Bridge—Highway 75 exit (Crosby Street) off I-5, no toll—and explore more of the island, whose best-kept secret is its beaches; they are not as popular with tourists as La Jolla or Pacific and Mission beaches, and so are less prone to crowding; their lovely white stretches of sand are also easy on the eyes.

You can travel south down Orange Avenue to reach the crown jewel of Coronado—the Hotel Del Coronado (1500 Orange Ave., Coronado, 800/HOTEL–DEL). The world-famous Victorian-era hotel and resort, built in 1888, has a white facade and red-spired roof that resemble a magical castle. The storybook-like exterior is well known from Billy Wilder's classic comedy film *Some Like It Hot*. The hotel is also reportedly haunted—Room 3312 is said to be

EATS FOR KIDS **Miguel's Cocina** (1351 Orange Ave., 619/437–4237) has Mexican fish tacos and chicken fajitas. Grab a quick sandwich or snack at the Hotel Del's Crown Market, **Splash Bar & Grill** or **Boardwalk Café**. And don't miss ice cream at **Moo Time Creamery** (1025 Orange Ave., 619/522–6890).

HEY, KIDS! Who was so enchanted by this place that he wrote a poem about it titled "Coronado, the Ocean of Fairyland"? It was Frank L. Baum, better known as the author of *The Wonderful Wizard of Oz*. He liked to vacation here in the wintertime (you can see his house at 1101 Star Park Circle). The architecture and towers of the Hotel Del Coronado reportedly served as Baum's inspiration for the design of Emerald City in the Oz books (he wrote 13 more!).

1100 Orange Ave. (visitor center)

Ferry $2 ages
4 and up

 Ferry 9–9; bridge open 24 hrs

619/437-8788

All ages

visited by the ghost of Kate Morgan, half of a husband-wife con artist team who, legend has it, was offed by her spouse not far from the hotel in 1892. She stayed in this room (then numbered 302), and her ghost has been spotted in the room's vicinity. Nonguests can stroll through the historic lobby, gardens, and along a newly refurbished boardwalk area that opens out toward the beach.

If you're driving and you head south on Highway 75 from the Hotel Del (as it's called by the locals), you'll learn another secret about Coronado—it's not really an island, it's connected to Imperial Beach in the south bay by a long narrow strip of land called the Silver Strand. The luxurious Loew's Coronado Bay Resort is here, and for a special treat, you can take the family for a gondola ride through the canals of the Coronado Cays (The Gondola Company, 619/429-6317; a 1-hr cruise runs about $90 for 4, includes hors d'oeuvres).

KEEP IN MIND   It's a delight to visit the Hotel Del Coronado during the holiday season. A highlight is the annual "Lighting of the Del" early in December, involving a 30-ft tree and some 50,000 lights. There are also two special period plays, *An American Christmas* and *Aunt Agatha's Christmas Tea*, performed by the local Lamb's Player's Theater (619/437-0600).

EAGLE AND HIGH PEAK MINES

46

Northern California gets all the glory for the gold rush, but there was gold in these here hills, too. Today, more than 150 years later, you still go into some of the original gold mines in the mountain town of Julian, about an hour northeast of San Diego, to see where miners found millions of dollars' worth of ore during the rush.

In 1869, Fred Coleman, a local rancher and one of the first African-American pioneers in the area, discovered flecks of gold in a creek near Julian, and San Diego County's only bona-fide gold rush was born. Many prospectors came to work the hard rock mines. Although the rush was over within a decade, Julian remains (see #43), and the Eagle and High Peak Mines can still be explored with a guide.

The hour-long tour takes you underground to the two interconnected mines. As you weave through the winding tunnels, passing antique machinery and rock displays, you'll hear about

KEEP IN MIND The 1,000-ft walk into the mines isn't too rigorous (there is one staircase). You'll be on a dirt path, so wear good walking shoes and nothing too precious, because you might get a little dusty. A light jacket is also a good idea. There are some low overhead spots where adults and taller kids will have to stoop. This trip is best for ambulatory kids (not good for strollers). When asked if the journey could be tackled by a grandmother, a staff person said, "Well, I don't know your grandmother, but if she's cranky, she can't come down here!"

 End of C St., Julian

 760/765-0036

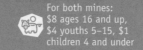 For both mines:
$8 ages 16 and up,
$4 youths 5–15, $1
children 4 and under

 Daily 10–2:30

 8 and up

the pioneers who settled the area. At one point the guide switches off the lights so you can see and hear—or not see and hear—how dark and quiet it is. Although this would be a cool place to yodel, speaking quietly in the mines is encouraged (loud noises and their echoes could exacerbate cave-ins over time), so this may not be the place to bring babies or toddlers, known for breaking into squeals or song without notice. At the end of the tour you'll get a demonstration on gold panning. The place was stripped of its wealth long ago, but there's no harm in looking for glitters while you're here. If you've still got the strength after the mines, consider some fishing at Lake Cuyamaca (*see #38*) or a visit to the California Wolf Center (*see #50*) while in Julian.

EATS FOR KIDS
The **Julian Café and Bakery** (2112 Main St., 760/765–2712), in a building dating from 1872, serves breakfast, lunch, and apple pie. Or, you can stop for a sandwich at the **Miner's Diner** (2134 Main St., 760/765–3753), and finish up with an ice-cream treat at their old-fashioned soda fountain afterward.

HEY, KIDS! Since the gold ran out here long ago, Julian could have become another ghost town (as many gold-rush towns did) but it had a secret weapon to keep it thriving—apples. Some of the region's first apple trees were planted here during the gold-rush days, and Julian is still renowned for its prizewinning apples. Citizens celebrate this heritage every fall at the Julian Apple Festival. And almost no one leaves Julian without taking home an apple pie from one of the town's many bakeries.

FERN STREET CIRCUS

ere's your chance to run away and join the circus. Well, you don't really have to run away—but for a couple of hours you *can* join the Fern Street Circus, and your kids can, too. This not-for-profit, community-based effort helps adults and kids fulfill big-top dreams by teaching circus skills.

Billing themselves as a theatrical and educational ensemble, the circus perpetually reminds neighbors and visitors that it's *always* in town with the Circus Skills after-school programs (offered throughout the country), performances, workshops, and day camps. The main Circus Skills program is run out of the Golden Hill Community Center, where you can immerse yourself in tumbling, juggling, clowning, contortion, tightwire, the trampoline, or trapeze. For resident kids, all this practicing culminates in a special "junior circus" recital each summer,

HEY, KIDS!
The circus as we know it today began in England in 1768 as a horse trick-riding show performed in a circular arena (this inspired the term "circus"). Acrobats, jugglers, and clowns were hired just to fill in the gaps between the horse performances.

EATS FOR KIDS At the **Turf Supper Club** (1116 25th St., 619/234–6363), established in 1950, you'll feel like you've entered one of the Rat Pack's hangouts. You'll get a grill in the middle of the table to cook your own beef or poultry. With all the sizzling and the proximity to the grill, this is a better bet for older kids. There's no lunch served, but you can come for dinner after your training session. For a late lunch before the session, stop by **Big Top Pizza** (1237 28th St., 619/234–9141, open 2–9) for pizza and lasagna.

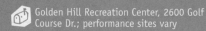 Golden Hill Recreation Center, 2600 Golf Course Dr.; performance sites vary

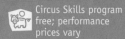 Circus Skills program free; performance prices vary

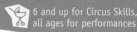 M 4–6 Circus Skills program; performance dates and times vary

619/235-9756; www.fernstreetcircus.org

6 and up for Circus Skills, all ages for performances

where they get to show off their new skills (adults get to show off in their own programs, too). Although instruction is offered free, the circus gratefully accepts donations.

If kids and teens who regularly train in the skills program show promise, they are often asked to join the main circus, composed of adult professional performers. Each year they create an entirely new and original show that is performed in Balboa Park for a two-week run (usually at the end of May). They also perform throughout the year at neighborhood fairs, the San Diego Street Scene, First Night in Escondido, and other venues. Everything at this circus is created by the member artists: the sets, the lighting, the costumes, the choreography, the narrative, and the music. The shows combine a rich mix of acrobatics and dance with a good dose of performance art. If you're lucky enough to be in town during a performance, don't miss it.

KEEP IN MIND The two-hour Circus Skills sessions are geared toward beginners. There are usually about 40 students at each session, and they move through the various stations to learn the skills. The instruction is highly supervised, and safety is strongly stressed (there have been few injuries since these sessions began in 1993). When you need a breather, just watch the other students and teachers tumble and juggle.

44

Hey—wanna catch some waves at the same beach where some of the world's gnarliest dudes perfected the art of surfing? Although I.B. (as it's known around here) may not be as famous as Malibu or Waikiki, it has its own important place in surfing history. Back in the 1940s when hanging ten was just becoming the rage, surfers flocked here for what were the largest waves in the United States at the time.

Although I.B. is still choice for hanging ten, it's also ideal for kids who are just hanging: the big waves have a gentle touch by the time they break at the shore, and the strip of sand isn't too wide, so you don't have to drag kids and toys too far to get to the water. Mostly locals come here, but to avoid crowds, it's best to arrive midmorning on weekdays. There's also a playground adjacent to the beach, Dunes Park (750 Seacoast Dr.), with slides,

KEEP IN MIND If you and your kids plan to catch some waves, please know your surfing etiquette. The surfer closest to the wave as it's breaking gets to own that wave (so don't speed up and try to get ahead of them . . . this is a big surfing no-no). And if someone is already riding a wave, never attempt to cut in front of them—it's bad manners and can cause a wipe-out for both of you.

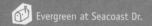 Evergreen at Seacoast Dr.

 Free

 Daily

 619/628-1362;
www.cityofib.com

 All ages

climbing areas, and picnic tables. Older kids might enjoy a walk over the ocean on the 1,500-ft Imperial Beach pier, and you can even fish here without a license.

Commemorating I.B.'s unique place in surf history is Surfhenge, a brilliantly colored sculpture inspired by the silhouettes of the surfboards the surfers would stick upright in the sand. The monument is at the entrance to Portwood Pier Plaza (10 Evergreen) that leads to the beach and the pier. Also have a look at the colorful benches on the plaza—yes, they look just like surfboards; each has a plaque detailing I.B.'s role in surfing history. I.B.'s other claim to fame is the U.S. Open Sandcastle Competition that it hosts each July, when life-size chess pieces, fantastic mermaids, and other amazing structures are created.

HEY, KIDS! If you're inspired to enter your own creation in the sandcastle competition, some of the permitted materials include seaweed, shells, water-based colors, flour, and sugar. And, of course, sand.

EATS FOR KIDS Head out to the end of the Imperial Beach Pier to the **Tin Fish** (910 Seacoast Dr., 619/628–8414) for chowders, seafood, chicken, and tacos. You can also eat right next door to the playground at Dunes Park at the **Beach Club Grille** (710 Seacoast Dr., 619/628–0777), which has sandwiches, burgers, and salads. The **IB Forum Sports Bar & Grill** (1079 Seacoast Dr., 619/429–7507) has a very reasonable children's menu that includes chicken tenders and grilled-cheese sandwiches.

JULIAN

San Diegans first started coming to Julian in 1869 to search for gold, and more than a century later they're still seeking out this town, but now for mountain getaways. Framed by winding, mountain roads and lush forests, Julian is a welcome change of scene for Southern California residents and visitors looking for a respite from busy freeways and endless urban sprawl.

Julian retains its gold rush heritage, and it's largely the town's pride in its history that makes it a fun place for kids. You can fill an hour or so at the Eagle and High Peak Mines (*see #46*) and then tour the old part of town, where many of the original buildings still stand and the flavor of the Old West endures.

Park for free on one of the side streets off Main Street; you can easily walk the several blocks that make up the downtown area. Begin your tour at the Julian Town Hall (2129 Main St.), which serves as a visitor center with resources and information on the area.

HEY, KIDS!
Most pioneers came to Julian for the gold, but town founder Drury Bailey stayed because he thought the land was so beautiful. He named the new town after his cousin Mike Julian, because he was the most handsome man in the area.

EATS FOR KIDS
So many apple pies, so little time. Start at the **Julian Pie Company** (2225 Main St., 760/765–2449), and then work your way through the **Apple Alley Bakery** (760/765–2532) and **Mom's Pies** (2119 Main St., 760/765–2472). You can get a burger with your pie at **Buffalo Bill's** (Third and Main, 760/765–1560), or steaks and seafood at the **Julian Grille** (2224 Main St., 760/760–0173). And no trip to Julian is complete without a stop at the **Julian Cider Mill** (2103 Main St., 760/765–1530) to pick up some of their apple cider, honey, dried fruit, and jams.

East of San Diego on Hwy. 78
at junction of Hwy. 79

Free; fee for some
attractions

Daily

760/765-1857
(Julian Chamber of Commerce)

All ages

Stroll along Main Street's wooden sidewalks, and then head down to the Julian Pioneer Museum (2811 Washington St., 760/765-0227) to show the kids a collection of artifacts that date from 1896 to 1913. You can also tour the town in an old-fashioned horse-drawn carriage (Country Carriages, 760/765-1471). If you visit during Julian Historic Days (the second weekend of the month, Jan–Sept) you'll get to see authentically costumed characters roaming the town, reenacting events from Julian's Wild West past, including gunfights.

Julian is nearly as famous for its apples as it is for its gold-mining heritage. There are several bakeries in town, each proudly selling its own version of the Julian Apple Pie. There is much dispute over which bakes the preeminent pie, so do your best to try as many as you can.

KEEP IN MIND Although most of the rest of the country has to struggle with it each winter, Southern Californians—spoiled rotten by near perfect weather year-round—go gaga over snow. Since snow is rare in San Diego proper—many kids here have never seen it up close—it's a treat to head up to Julian in wintertime, stop by the side of the road, and let them have a snowball fight, go sledding, or make snow angels.

KNOTT'S SOAK CITY U.S.A.

With so many beaches, bay fronts, and lakes in San Diego County, you'd think a water park wouldn't pack that much appeal. But kids love Knott's Soak City. The water is a little more playful here, whether it's drenching them from above, shooting up at them from below, or propelling them down a slide.

The 22 water rides and attractions at this 32-acre park are particular hits with elementary school–age kids and teens. Your thrill seekers will want to try Palisades Plunge, Imperial Run, Solana Storm, Watch Tower, and La Jolla Falls—combined, these offer 16 tube, body, and speed slides that shoot riders down rushing streams of water to pools below. It's kind of a cross between a long slide and a roller coaster, except there are no seats and they get totally soaked. Another favorite is the three-story Beach House, filled with water cannons, climbing nets, and a gigantic bucket that refills itself every few minutes and then topples over to soak everyone below.

HEY, KIDS! What do a water park and boysenberries have in common? Back in the 1930s a man named Rudolph Boysen created a new kind of berry from strains of raspberries, blackberries, and loganberries, but his plants kept dying. Then farmer Walter Knott figured out how to nurture the plants and make them thrive. He started selling the boysenberries—which he named after their originator—at his local farm stand, and they were a hit. That stand blossomed into what's now the Knott's Berry Farm theme park, which in turn inspired Soak City.

2052 Entertainment Circle,
Chula Vista

619/661-7373;
www.knotts.com/soakcity

$22.95 ages
12 and up, $15.95
children 3–11;
parking $6

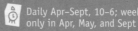
Daily Apr–Sept, 10–6; weekends
only in Apr, May, and Sept

2 and up

There are attractions here designed especially for littler kids, such as Gremmie Lagoon, a 4-ft-deep kids' water playground. Tyke's Trough is for the tiniest guppies—it's a shallower wading pool with little slides (the park offers free life vests to use upon request).

You get to play here, too. You can float down the lazy Sparkletts Sunset River in an inner tube, or relax in the lapping, gentle waves of the 500,000-gallon Balboa Bay wave pool as you splash with your toddlers in the shallow end. Then load the whole family into one of the rafts on the Coronado Express and take the 688-ft half-pipe tube ride together. Bring along sunscreen and reapply, reapply, reapply (it tends to come off with all the sliding and splashing), or you'll be going home with sore little red lobsters.

EATS FOR KIDS
The park has lots of kids' favorites: pizza at **Surf Daddies**, hot dogs at **Salty Dogs**, tacos at **Casa Ortega**, and hamburgers and ribs at **Long Board Eats**. There are also food carts throughout the park for drinks, cotton candy, ice cream, and popcorn.

KEEP IN MIND Just next door is the Coors Amphitheatre, the largest pop concert facility in San Diego County, with seating for 22,000. For appropriate shows, the outdoor theater is especially family friendly because of its lawn seating area, where kids have the freedom to move around. There are also large video screens so they won't miss the action on stage. The theater shares a parking lot with Soak City, which makes sense, as they are open at opposite times (2050 Entertainment Circle, 619/671–3600).

LA JOLLA COVE

41

This isn't your typical "surf's up" type of beach so often associated with Southern California, but rather, a romantic, rugged, sublime part of the coastline, the kind with windswept cliffs that you see in your mind's eye when you read great novels set by the sea. This is the beach as art.

Your kids, however, will most likely enjoy coming here to run free in the green Ellen Browning Scripps Park atop the beach cliff, or to go to the intimate, sheltered beach carved into the cliff side below. The waves are gentle, the beach boulders are suitable for climbing, and your kids can watch divers in full gear as they go out to explore the San Diego La Jolla Underwater Park Ecological Reserve just offshore. You'll all want to check out the Children's Pool (850 Coast Blvd.), which is for looking, not swimming; although this sea wall-protected area was initially created so that children would have a safe place to swim, local seals and sea lions liked it so much that they adopted it as their own swimming and sunning spot.

EATS FOR KIDS **Goldfish Point Café** (1255 Coast Blvd., 858/459–7407) has fresh soup, sandwiches, and pizza. For a spectacular view of the water, go up to **Azul** (1250 Prospect St., 858/454–9616), casually elegant with a tapas lunch and a children's menu that includes chicken, fish, and pasta.

HEY, KIDS! Just like at land-based nature preserves, the animals and plants at the San Diego La Jolla Underwater Park Ecological Reserve are protected, so they can't be caught, collected, or harmed. This is good news for the harbor seals, sea lions, leopard sharks, and other sea creatures that live in the 533 protected acres here under the sea. If you visit the Birch Aquarium (see #54) you can see what the reserve looks like underwater, because it's recreated in the kelp forest exhibit.

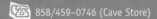 1100 Coast Blvd., La Jolla

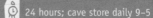 858/459-0746 (Cave Store)

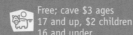 Free; cave $3 ages 17 and up, $2 children 16 and under

 24 hours; cave store daily 9–5

All ages

Older kids might be interested in knowing that there are seven caves tucked into the coast just north of here. Although most are not easily accessible, you can walk right down into the "Sunny Jim" cave through the Cave Store (1325 Coast Blvd.), descending 144 steps. The cave was named after a popular late-19th-century comic character because the outline of its opening to the sea resembles his profile.

While you're in the neighborhood, visit the nearby Museum of Contemporary Art San Diego (*see #31*). Just up the coast is another spectacular beach ideal for swimming, La Jolla Shores (*see #40*). Also don't miss the Birch Aquarium at Scripps (*see #54*) a few miles north for a look at what's in the water in La Jolla.

GETTING THERE La Jolla Cove is a very popular spot in the summer, so parking here can be frustrating. It's best to come on weekday mornings. There is street parking at the cove, but it fills up quickly. You can park on the residential streets in the village of La Jolla (it's not too far to walk down to the cove from there), but you may want to save time and your sanity and spring for paid parking; most convenient is the Ace Parking lot at 1231 Cave St. ($1.75 per half hour), or call Ace (858/454–8559) for other locations.

40

L a Jolla Shores is that rare beach in Southern California that has it all—soft sand and gentle surf, plus extras such as a large grassy park, a playground, a boardwalk for strolling, and lifeguards. It's also on one of the most stunning parts of the coast in storybook-beautiful La Jolla. No wonder it's one of San Diego's most desirable beaches for families.

Because it's so popular with locals and tourists, the Shores can get busy, especially in summer. Your best bet is to arrive early, and you can easily plan on spending the day. Toddlers through elementary school–age kids can start out in the playground next to the beach; they'll see rolling waves and seagulls as they swing back and forth, and they'll love spinning down the slide into soft, white sand. Kellogg Park, with its carpet of grass, is also good for running, kite flying, Frisbee, or volleyball. You can picnic here, too—there are tables and even a

EATS FOR KIDS For a sit-down meal with a great view of the beach, try the **Shores Restaurant at the Sealodge** (just south of the beach at 8110 Camino del Oro, 858/456–0600) with an extensive children's menu (including cheeseburgers and popcorn shrimp) and patio seating. You can get a quick lunch at **Jeff's Burgers** (2152 Avenida de la Playa, 858/454–8038) or Mexican food at **La Jolla Cantina** (2161 Avenida de la Playa, 858/459–5282). For picnic supplies, try the **La Jolla Shores Market** (2259 Avenida de la Playa, 858/459–3465).

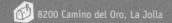 8200 Camino del Oro, La Jolla

 Free

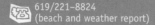 619/221-8824
(beach and weather report)

 Daily, 24 hrs

 All ages

few barbecues to use. As the day heats up, head across the sand to the beach. The waves here are notoriously calm, so even the littlest kids can get their toes wet. Older children can swim, Boogie Board, body surf, or just soak up some sun. For the more adventurous, there are kayaks to rent. You can also sign up for scuba lessons to peek at the sea life in the San Diego La Jolla Underwater Park Ecological Reserve.

Try to stick around for a walk along the beach at sunset. Then, end your day with a San Diego beach tradition—a bonfire in one of the fire pits. Don't forget to bring marshmallows!

KEEP IN MIND Can't hack an entire day at the beach? Just wash off the sand at the showers here and head to some other La Jolla attractions, including Birch Aquarium (see #54), La Jolla Cove (see #41), and the Museum of Contemporary Art.

GETTING THERE The only downside to visiting this lovely beach is parking and traffic. The Shores has its own free parking lot, but it often fills up by midday, so you can also park for free in the surrounding neighborhood. The main route into La Jolla (Ardath Road off I–5) can get congested. Instead, take I–805 to the La Jolla Village Drive/Miramar Road exit. Head west on La Jolla Village Drive, which becomes North Torrey Pines Road; bear left at Expedition Way, make a right on Downwind Way, and go left onto La Jolla Shores Drive; Kellogg Park and the Shores will be on your right.

LA MESA VILLAGE

Walking the old downtown La Mesa village is like strolling through a small hometown, but, surprisingly, it's right in the middle of sprawling San Diego County, about 11 mi east of busy downtown San Diego.

Start your visit at the Old La Mesa Train Depot (4695 Nebo Dr.). Though the train doesn't run through here anymore, some of it is still parked here, so the kids can climb aboard and explore as they watch the "modern" version (the San Diego Trolley) fly by on adjacent tracks. As part of the San Diego Railroad Museum, the depot has been restored to its 1915 condition, and you can tour the ticketing and waiting area, the telegrapher's station, and the exhibit in the baggage room for free on weekend afternoons. You'll also get to visit the steam locomotive and freight cars here, but the kids can explore from the outside anytime.

GETTING THERE It's an easy trip here from downtown San Diego if you take the Orange Line of the San Diego Trolley. The ride takes around 40 minutes and costs about $2.25 per person. This trolley is the only convenient way to get here other than driving; buses do run from downtown San Diego, but that could take hours and many transfers.

EATS FOR KIDS The **Village Garden Restaurant** (8384 La Mesa Blvd., 619/462–9100) is a favorite local spot for lunch or breakfast, and you can consume your bakery items and sandwiches in the garden. **Sanfilippo's Pizza** (8141 La Mesa Blvd., 619/464–2088) has been a fixture here for many years, serving up good Italian fare. And one of the very best Mexican food restaurants in all of San Diego County is right here in La Mesa Village: **Mario's de la Mesa** (8425 La Mesa Blvd., 619/461–9390) has fresh, authentic, delicious entrees—be sure to try the *carnitas* (braised pork).

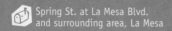 Spring St. at La Mesa Blvd. and surrounding area, La Mesa

 619/462-3000; www.lvma.com

 Free; fees for some services

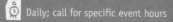 Daily; call for specific event hours

 All ages

The downtown village area continues several blocks both east and west from the intersection of La Mesa Boulevard at Spring Street. The family will enjoy browsing the quaint storefronts, and you might want to grab a quick bite or stop in at Yellow Book Road (*see #1*). If everyone's up to it, also explore the nearby residential streets to see the Victorian-era homes (rarities in San Diego). The village is busy with special events year-round: Thursday evenings there's a classic car show (April–September). A farmer's market with fruit, vegetables, flowers, and other goodies is held from 3 to 6 every Friday afternoon. Flag Day is celebrated with an old-fashioned parade each year. And during the holidays, you can experience "Christmas in the Village" with crafts, caroling, and pony rides. But La Mesa's biggest annual event is Oktoberfest—it draws crowds nearing 200,000!

KEEP IN MIND Oktoberfest is held on the first weekend of October, and admission is free. The village closes off to traffic and the streets fill with music, rides, crafts, and food. Be sure to take the kids into the Bavarian-style beer garden area for live German music performances and the chance to polka. You'll also learn how to perform what has become a favorite wedding spectacle, the Chicken Dance, especially entertaining when the dancers are wearing lederhosen.

LAKE CUYAMACA

It's well worth trekking to this mountain getaway about 40 mi east of San Diego. In a large clearing among the pine and oak forests of the Peninsular Mountain Range, Lake Cuyamaca stretches over 110 acres, and there's a lot to do. You can rent a boat on the lake, picnic, hike, and feed the ducks. You might very well spy other wildlife here, too, as more than 200 species of birds, deer, squirrels, chipmunks, jackrabbits, and even mountain lions live in the area.

If you're angling for something slightly different there's a free fishing class held every Saturday at 10 AM where your kids will learn about casting and the nitty-gritty of rigging tackle and lures, and baiting a hook. Later, they will have the opportunity to try for some of the bass, trout, channel catfish, and other fish regularly stocked at the lake. This might also be the time to haul out the saying, "That's why they call it fishing and not catching."

HEY, KIDS! What's a "cuyamaca" anyway? Is it the name of a tree? Or some weird geographical formation? Actually, it's based on a name that was given to this area by the native Kumeyaay people who lived here thousands of years ago—they called it "Ah-Ha Kwe-Ah Mac," which loosely translates to "the place where it rains." Spanish speakers who later passed through this area modified the name to its current "Cuyamaca."

 15027 Hwy. 79, Julian

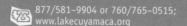 877/581-9904 or 760/765-0515; www.lakecuyamaca.org

 Fishing $5 adults, $2.50 children; one-day fishing license $10.75 (mandatory for ages 16 and up); parking $6; other fees vary

 Daily 6 AM–sunset

 All ages; fishing 5 and up

If camping's your thing, there are a few sites next to the lake, available on a first come, first served basis, so get here early if your heart is set on sleeping lakeside. The lake is surrounded by Cuyamaca Rancho State Park, which has campgrounds and more than 100 mi of trails for hikers, bikers, and equestrians. The closest campground to the lake is 2 mi away at Paso Picacho (800/444-7275); it has 85 sites and five cabins. Here you'll also find many hiking trails, such as the Paso Nature Trail, an easy hike for kids at a half mile each way. Another good spot is the idyllic, 900-acre William Heise County Park (4945 Heise Park Rd., Julian, 858/694-3049), with RV and tent sites and cabins, and evening programs on nature, fire prevention, and astrology. Consider combining a visit to Cuyamaca with a side trip to nearby Julian (see #43).

EATS FOR KIDS The **Lake Cuyamaca Restaurant** (760/765-0700), next to the bait shop at the lake, offers a hearty meal before a day full of fishing and hiking. Or, go up the road to the **Lakeland Resort** (14916 Hwy. 79, 760/765-0736) for such dishes as chicken and prime rib.

KEEP IN MIND Even though the mountain lions in the area are fairly elusive, a few safety tips couldn't hurt on the off-chance that you should encounter one: Whatever you do, don't run, because this just sparks the lions' hunting instincts. It's best to stand tall and face them. Try to make yourself look bigger by raising your arms and fanning out your jacket. If the lions get aggressive, fight back by throwing rocks and sticks (it's a good idea to carry a walking stick while hiking).

LAKE MURRAY

37

If you're not up for heading to the mountains or the country just to find a lake, meet Lake Murray, improbably situated in a ring of homes and businesses smack in the middle of San Diego County. In this 160-acre urban oasis—it's a man-made reservoir created about a century ago—you can hike, ogle birds, take out a motorboat, pedal boat, or canoe, or just stroll part of the lake's 3-mi trail.

A favorite activity transcending all age groups is feeding the ducks—and there are plenty here to nourish right from the shore. Just bring along some stale bread and they will follow you anywhere you go around the lake (some of them can be a little aggressive, so be prepared if your littler ones aren't pleased by the chase). The paved path that edges the lake's perimeter

HEY, KIDS!

Lake Murray may be artificial, but it serves as a home to plenty of fish, ducks, birds, and plants. It was created to collect and store water for the people of San Diego. The reservoir still yields drinking water, though it's processed first at a water filtration plant in nearby Alvarado.

EATS FOR KIDS The **Lake Murray Concession Stand** (in the main parking lot) has hot breakfasts and lunches—eggs and burgers dominate, respectively—as well as snacks and sundries. Just before the main entrance to the lake is the **Gold Star Taco Shop**, at the corner of Kiowa and Lake Murray Boulevard. Or, drive north on Lake Murray Boulevard a couple of blocks to **La Mesa Ocean Grill and Seafood Market** (5465 Lake Murray Blvd., 619/463–1548) for seafood wraps and crab cake sandwiches. There are also 64 picnic tables and 10 barbecues to use at the lake.

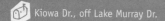 Kiowa Dr., off Lake Murray Dr.

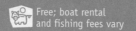 Free; boat rental and fishing fees vary

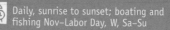 Daily, sunrise to sunset; boating and fishing Nov–Labor Day, W, Sa–Su

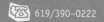 619/390-0222

 All ages

makes a great trail and is wide enough to accommodate strollers; older kids can ride their bikes, scooters, and Rollerblades here, too. Although the trail follows most of the lake, it does end at a dam, so you'll need to turn around and head back the way you came. It's about a 3-mi trek each way, so do as much or as little as your group can endure.

There's no swimming here, but you can fish from the shore for bass, bluegill, channel catfish, crappie, or trout (there's a five-fish limit on all of these except for crappie—you can keep up to 25 of those). And to enjoy more of San Diego's natural landscape, venture to nearby Mission Trails Regional Park (*see #32*), where you can hike through an enormous preserve and learn about regional flora and fauna at the visitor center.

GETTING THERE Lake Murray is about 10 mi east of downtown San Diego, surrounded by three cities: San Diego, La Mesa, and Santee. To get to the main entrance, take I–8 west to the Lake Murray Boulevard exit and then turn (left) on Kiowa Drive. You can also access it from Lake Murray Community Park (7051 Murray Park Dr.), plus there's a playground here. For access with a great view of the lake, park on the west side of Baltimore Drive (between Bertro Drive and El Paso Street) and head down the stairs toward the lake.

LEGOLAND CALIFORNIA

Toddlers and preschoolers longing for theme park thrills at their speed may just find them here; Legoland California is jammed with things they can touch, climb on, and drive, as well as gaze at with awe, as many of the fanciful structures are constructed from Lego bricks.

It'll take 45 minutes to get here from San Diego, but you'll be rewarded by 128 fun-filled acres. Your preschoolers will enjoy riding colorful boats, helicopters, airplanes, and cars while traveling through fantasy lands filled with giant Lego animals, such as a smoke-breathing dragon and 18-ft-tall giraffes. The bricks also dazzle in miniature in the Mini-World area, which exhibits tiny yet detailed re-creations of American cities, including San Diego.

Kids 10–12 might get a kick out of the Lego Technic Coasters, the Aquazone Wave Racers, and the LEGO Racers 4-D interactive movie. Children 2–12 seem to enjoy Hideaways on

HEY, KIDS! Does looking at all of these Lego bricks make you want to build something? No problem! Legoland has plenty of places where you can put together your own creations: you can check out the Builder's Guild in Castle Hill, or head over to Road and Test in the Imagination Zone. There's even a Duplo Play place here so toddlers and preschoolers can build, too. Kids 10 and older are invited to sign up to build exclusive computerized robots known as Lego Mindstorms.

 One Legoland Dr., Carlsbad

 760/918-LEGO;
www.legoland.com

 $39.95 ages 17
and up, $33.95 children
3–16; parking $8

 Daily 10–5; hours vary seasonally

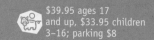 2–12

Castle Hill, a giant, mazelike climbing structure, as well as the Driving School; you won't find automated cars on a track here—these are real, independently moving Lego-style cars, with accelerators and brakes, that kids ages 6–12 can drive. The 3–5-year-olds get their shot, too, at the Junior Driving School next door. And everybody gets their own "driver's license" to take home. You can ride with your kids everywhere except the Driving School and on Royal Joust, a horse ride.

Don't miss a chance to stroll through the Lego Factory in Fun Town, as it shows how all those little bricks are made. Then tour the nearby Adventurers Club to see the clever re-creations of Egyptian artifacts (though moving objects in here might scare some younger kids).

EATS FOR KIDS

Fun Town Market has something for everyone with stir-fry, pasta, sandwiches, and salads. For pizza, go to **Ristorante Brickolini.** Burgers, hot dogs, and snacks can be found at kiosks throughout the park. For fresh fruit stop at **The Market** near the park entrance.

KEEP IN MIND
It might seem like you and your wallet are walking into the lion's den by entering a theme park based on a line of toys, so prepare for the barrage of souvenir requests by budgeting a little extra money. Of course, you don't have to give in to the buying frenzy (bless you for your strength!)—just keep the kids busy in the Lego building areas and their "free" Lego driver's license can serve as a souvenir. When you see some of the appealing items sold here, though, you might be the one who requires some restraint.

MAGDALENA ECKE YMCA SKATE PARK

The extreme skateboarding culture began right here in Southern California ("So Cal" in local lingo) when a few dudes felt the need to ride their skateboards up the sides of empty swimming pools and down the handrails of steep staircases. Luckily for property owners those prime skateboarding experiences are now reproduced at specially designed skate parks like this one, where you can see how today's young So Cal skaters are pushing the sport to the next level.

This 33,000-sq-ft wooden park has all the things the "new school" skaters need to execute *ollies* and *kickflips* while riding the *half-pipe* (*see* HEY, KIDS! box *below* for translations). Some of these kids seem to defy gravity as they take on the street course here packed with ramps, pyramids, handrail stations, and miniramps with spines (for *grinding*). And for added coolness, the famous 80-ft-wide by 13-ft-high *vert* (vertical ramp) here was designed by

EATS FOR KIDS **Oggi's Pizza** (305 Encinitas Blvd., 760/944–8170) has pasta, calzone, salads, and pizza (and a children's menu). The nearby **Coco's Bakery Restaurant** (407 Encinitas Blvd., 760/436–6023) has burgers and sandwiches.

KEEP IN MIND Visitors as well as locals are welcome to participate at these parks, but this obviously could be a problem if you're not traveling with wheels, and the park doesn't rent them. Should you have your own gear with you or have the opportunity to borrow some, be aware that the parks strictly enforce safety, so the kids will need helmets and elbow and knee pads, and the BMXers will need shin guards. Also, park guidelines state that "gnarly behavior is not tolerated." Be prepared to sign a medical release form, too. Sessions run about 2½ hours each; call for start times.

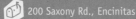 200 Saxony Rd., Encinitas

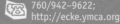 760/942-9622;
http://ecke.ymca.org

 Free for spectators; participant
sessions $10 nonmembers,
$6 members (weekends),
$4 members (weekdays);
$30 annual membership

 M–F 3:15–8, Sa–Su 9–5

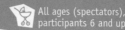 All ages (spectators),
participants 6 and up

a nearby resident, skating legend Tony Hawk, who's been known to skate here from time to time. If Tony's name sounds only vaguely familiar, know that he has probably already been to your house or the neighbor's in his wildly popular video game incarnation (and you can check out highlights of his career at the Hall of Champions (*see #22*).

Bicycle stunts will likely please your whole brood, so head over to the nearby 23,000-sq-ft BMX Dirt Jump Park. Although it might look like gigantic piles of dirt to you, it's just the place to watch the BMX crowd ride and go on to master the jumps, roll-ins, banks and rhythm sections, lips, gaps, and transfers found in the intermediate through pro sections. You're welcome to watch all the action in these parks for free, as long as you stay behind the fences, safely out of the way of speeding boards and bikes.

HEY, KIDS! Here's some skateboarding lingo that might come in handy (please pass this on to your confused parents). *Deck*: standing surface of the skateboard. *Trucks*: parts that hold the wheels to the board's underside. *Grind*: sliding along a surface's edge on the trucks. *Half-pipe*: a U-shaped ramp. *Ollie*: a jump that entails tapping the tail end of the board onto the ground. *Kickflip*: kicking the board into a spin in the air before landing on it with your feet. *Air*: riding with all wheels off the ground. *Slam*: to fall (for your parents' sake, try to avoid this one).

MARIE HITCHCOCK PUPPET THEATER

The mere mention of puppetry or ventriloquism doesn't generate much excitement among young audiences today, and it's a shame. Although Shari Lewis videos and *Sesame Street* can get kids excited about these arts, there's really no substitute for the simple delight that a good old-fashioned puppet show can elicit from children.

Marie Hitchcock is "the longest running puppet theater in America" (more than 50 years of shows) and one of the last of its kind in California. It began as the Puppet Theater in Balboa Park, and was later renamed in honor of local marionette "puppet lady" Marie Hitchcock, who performed here for 45 years.

The shows, performed five days a week, incorporate marionettes, hand puppets, rod puppets, shadow puppets, and ventriloquism. Members of the San Diego Puppetry Guild as well as visiting artists and troupes do the shows, ranging from traditional fairy tales such

HEY, KIDS! A marionette is a puppet moved with strings. But how did it get its name? Stringed puppets are some of the oldest kind, dating back at least as far as ancient Greece and Rome. But the name probably came about in the Middle Ages, when the Christian Church used puppetry plays to spread their beliefs. It is believed that the name "marionette," which means "little Mary," may have come from the stringed puppet that depicted the Virgin Mary in a popular play about the birth of Jesus.

2130 Pan American Rd.,
Palisades Bldg.

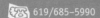
619/685-5990

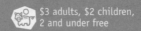
$3 adults, $2 children,
2 and under free

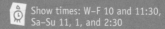
Show times: W–F 10 and 11:30,
Sa–Su 11, 1, and 2:30

2–9

as "Jack and the Beanstalk" to original stories to comedy, pantomime, music shows, and holiday reviews.

Programs change weekly at the 230-seat theater. Shows, most less than an hour, are perfect for preschool and young elementary school kids. Babies ought to be able to stick with most of it, and older kids will probably roll their eyes . . . but secretly enjoy the show. And parents—well, we typically have the biggest grins, along with a few nostalgia-induced tears.

A lovely grass-filled park area just outside of the theater is a perfect place to allow the kids to blow off some steam either before or after the show. It's also a good spot for picnicking. In the nearby Pan American Plaza parking lot you can hop a free tram to explore the rest of Balboa Park (*see #59*).

(*see #59*)

EATS FOR KIDS
After reliving your youth at the puppet theater, it would be fitting to try **The Chicken Pie Shop** (2633 El Cajon Blvd., 619/295–0156), which has served hot chicken pot pies since 1938. Sides include mashed potatoes and green beans, and, if you finish your vegetables, banana cream pie.

KEEP IN MIND Just north of the puppet theater is the House of Pacific Relations (619/234–0739), a charming group of little cottages, each representing one of more than 30 different nations, including Argentina, China, Hungary, and Scotland. They host an open house here on Sunday from 12 to 5 (March to October) that includes special lawn programs with food, crafts, costumes, folk music, and dancing (performances are usually at 2). Be sure to bring along change and small bills, because some of the houses offer sample tastes for modest donations.

MISSION BAY

There's something just a little different about the beach areas along Mission Bay Park. The water in this sheltered bay is gentle, without waves that will topple the littler ones. The parkland ringing the bay front is jammed with trees, picnic areas, and playgrounds, as well as 20 mi of paved pathways perfect for strolling, bicycling, and rollerblading. And, because it's a whopping 4,600 acres, different areas of the bay have been set aside specifically for swimming, boating, waterskiing, and fishing.

There are several playgrounds scattered around the bay, but the one at Tecolote Shores Park (1600 E. Mission Bay Dr.) is one of the best in San Diego. It has a blend of older (circa 1960s) and newer (circa 1990s) climbing structures, swings, large areas of white sand, and a "ship" to explore, plus it's designed to accommodate kids of all ages and abilities. The

EATS FOR KIDS **Rubio's Baja Grill** is legendary for fish tacos, and they have a kids' menu (4504 Mission Bay Dr., 619/272–2801); the food's portable enough to bring to the bay for a picnic. Or pick up some burgers and fries at **In-N-Out Burger** (2910 Damon Ave., 800/786–1000).

KEEP IN MIND The bay's calm water is conducive to wading with toddlers as long as you're mindful of the steep drop-off just off shore. The point of the drop-off varies in different spots (and changes with the tide); it can be anywhere from 4 to about 15-ft out, so it's best to test the water depth yourself first. The deeper water provides a perfect saltwater "pool" for older, strong swimmers to enjoy.

 Many areas are accessible from Mission Bay Dr. (off I-5)

  Free

 Daily, 24 hrs

 619/221-8899

All ages

only downside is that the park's immense size and proximity to the water makes it hard to keep an eye on more than one kid at a time, so if possible, come with more than one grown-up to assist with coverage.

Teens and 'tweens can try out water sports on the bay, and there are several places where you can rent Jet Skis, Wave Runners, motorboats, catamarans, sailboards, kayaks, and Aqua-Cycles). Rentals run hourly to daily, and prices range from about $15 per hour for an Aqua-Cycle to $150 for a water-ski boat with instructor and skis. Two places to try are CP Watersports (1775 E. Mission Bay Dr., 619/275-8945) and Seaforth Mission Bay (1641 Quivera Rd., 619/233-1681). You can rent bicycles and Rollerblades, too.

GETTING THERE Mission Bay is bordered by Mission Bay Drive to the east, Mission Beach to the west, Grand Avenue to the north, and Sea World Drive to the south. For other parks with playgrounds try Leisure Lagoon (1900 E. Mission Bay Dr.) or Sail Bay (4000 Fanuel St.). Boat rentals can be found near Bonita Cove and Ventura Cove (1000 W. Mission Bay Dr.). To water-ski, head to Ski Beach (2900 Ingraham at Vacation Rd.).

MISSION TRAILS REGIONAL PARK

Long before Father Junipero Serra showed up in the area to build the first of California's missions, the land here was inhabited by the native Kumeyaay people. It's believed they lived in villages along this river gorge a thousand years ago. It's well worth the trip here to see what the region looked like to these people then, as this park is protected and remains wild—and it's a mere 8 mi east of busy downtown San Diego.

Also here is a historic monument, the Old Mission Dam, built in the early 19th century to bring water to Serra's Mission San Diego de Alcala, just a few miles west of here. You can hike to the dam (about 1½ mi), but it's much easier to drive there. It has educational placards, and the kids can explore the generous pathway that leads to an overlook of the dam.

KEEP IN MIND You can take the kids wilderness camping at the Kumeyaay Lake Campground (619/668–2748) without having to leave the city. There are both RV and tent campsites here. Special campground programs are also available, including night hikes, campfire programs, animal tracking classes, guided trail walks, a star party, native plant walks, and crafts for kids ages 3 and up. The Kids Night Out program includes a cookout, marshmallow roast, crafts, and campfire stories.

 One Father Junipero Serra Trail

 Free

 Daily 9–5 (Visitor and Interpretive Center)

 619/668–3275; www.mtrp.org

2 and up

There are nearly 5,800 acres of open land and many miles of trails to explore here for all levels of hikers, including a paved road that's perfect for strollers. You can hike the trails on your own or take a guided nature walk—they leave the center each Saturday, Sunday, and Wednesday at 9:30 (best for kids 8 and older). But even a trip to the visitor center is a worthy activity. It has soaring windows with grand views of the park and plenty of exhibits that the kids can touch and see. On the second floor and its patio there are telescopes they can use to take a closer look at the grounds. They'll also get a kick out of walking up the long ramp to the second-floor exhibits, as it becomes a passageway filled with the sounds of the nocturnal animals that live here.

EATS FOR KIDS
On the way to the park, stop for lunch at **Rice Jones** (6618 Mission Gorge Rd., 619/528–8301) for Vietnamese and California fare. Or, on the way home, have dinner at **Pinnacle Peak Steakhouse** (7927 Mission Gorge Rd., 619/448–8882), a fun, Wild West–style place with reasonable prices.

HEY, KIDS! The Kumeyaay people reportedly first came to Southern California from the Colorado River area about 2,000 years ago. (They once inhabited most of San Diego County and parts of the Anza Borrego Desert and Imperial Valley, too.) Although there aren't any Kumeyaay still living in this park, there are plenty in the county. The Mission Trails region is now under the jurisdiction of the Viejas Band of Kumeyaay, who are known for their community work and for their popular casino and outlet center near Alpine. Want to say "hello" in the Kumeyaay language? It's *howka*.

MUSEUM OF CONTEMPORARY ART SAN DIEGO

If you're reluctant to miss one bit of Southern California's obnoxiously perfect weather, know that some of the top attractions at the Museum of Contemporary Art are outside. For starters, the building is on a sloping hillside with a spectacular view of the ocean. Also setting the scene is the Edwards Sculpture Garden, filled with whimsical works that look more like playground accessories than outdoor gallery pieces. The kids will especially enjoy the giant, cookie cutter–like figures made from grass, dirt, and concrete (Vito Acconci's "Displaced Person"), and Niki de Saint Phalle's large, colorful, creature-like sculpture, "Big Ganesh." Another must-see is Ramon de Salvo's "Liquid Ballistic": it looks like a cannon protecting the coastline, but you'll be delighted to discover that it functions in an entirely different way.

It's worth dragging yourself inside the museum, too. The 3,000-piece collection spans art movements since 1950 and includes work by Warhol, Holzer, Irwin, and Goldsworthy.

EATS FOR KIDS The **Museum Café** here has soups, sandwiches, salads, and drinks (858/456–6427). It's open weekdays 11–3, weekends 10–5. In a pinch you can also tuck into a stack of Funny-Faced Pancakes at the **International House of Pancakes** just down the street (811 Prospect St., 858/511–9775).

GETTING THERE Take the scenic route into La Jolla (pronounced La Hoi-ya)—I–5 north from San Diego, exiting on Ardath Road. At Torrey Pines Road make a slight left. Then turn right on Prospect, stay in the right lane, and go down hilly Cave Street, which veers left to become Coast Boulevard (check out the great ocean view from here). Continue on and head left toward Coast Boulevard South. Turn right on Girard Avenue, and make a slight right onto Prospect Street, and the museum will be a few blocks down on the right side.

 700 Prospect St., La Jolla

 $6 ages 19 and up,
$2 children 12–18; 1st Su
and 3rd T of mth free

 M, T, F, Sa–Su 11–5, Th 11–7

 858/454–3541;
www.mcasandiego.org

All ages

About a dozen exhibits mounted annually include works by Ellsworth Kelly, John Baldessari, and Christo as well as shows focusing on Latin American and California artists. There are guided tours offered Tuesday and weekends at 2 and 3, and Thursday at 6 and 7.

Of special interest are the Free-for-All First Sundays, held on the first Sunday of every month. There are art-making activities for the kids (and adults)—such as designing furniture or making sculptures—inspired by the current exhibition. The museum also has artist demonstrations and entertainment, including music, dance, and circus performances, and it's always fun, festive, and free—as is admission to the museum during the events.

For more art, visit the museum's other exhibition space in downtown San Diego (1001 Kettner Blvd., 619/234–1001) open daily 11–5 (but closed Wednesday), admission free.

HEY, KIDS! Have you wondered what makes some art contemporary? It's really all relative. Some of the art in this museum dates back to 1950, which is really not a long time in terms of art history. Some of the first art discovered was made by Paleolithic humans, like the paintings of horses, deer, and other animals found on the walls of caves in Lascaux, France. This early art is believed to be about 17,000 years old!

OLD TOWN SAN DIEGO STATE HISTORIC PARK

Just a little northeast of downtown San Diego, Old Town is the most-visited state park in California. This may be because it's still a vital part of the community, and just as many locals as tourists come here to enjoy the restaurants and shops. But Old Town is also where San Diego and, in fact, all of California began—it was the first European settlement in the territory because of its proximity to the first of Father Junipero Serra's missions, established east of here just up the hill in 1769 (Mission San Diego de Alcala was moved, destroyed, and rebuilt several times, and you'll now find it at 10818 San Diego Mission Road about 6 mi inland from here).

Old Town covers several blocks, and some parts have been closed to cars, so it's a nice place to explore on foot (and with strollers). Older kids can get into the history of the

EATS FOR KIDS Finding good food in Old Town is no problem, as long as you like Mexican fare. One of the most beautiful restaurants is **Casa de Bandini** (2660 Calhoun St., 619/297–8211). Be sure to eat outside on the patio courtyard, where you can enjoy the colorful flowers and the strolling mariachis' music. For something a little different, try authentic dishes from Mexico's Veracruz, Yucatan, and Mexico City regions at **El Agave** (2304 San Diego Ave., 619/220–0692). **Berta's Latin American Restaurant** (3928 Twiggs, 619/295–2343) has food from Colombia, Peru, Argentina, and other parts of South America.

 San Diego Ave. and Twiggs St.

 Free

 Daily 10–5

 619/220–5422

All ages

area. Take them around to the historic buildings to get a glimpse of what life was like here in the 19th century. They can visit original adobes, an old one-room school, a blacksmith's shop, and even a haunted house (*see #6*). If you come here on Wednesday from 10 to 2 you'll see costumed docents throughout the park presenting living history demonstrations of crafts, cooking, music, and blacksmithing (on the fourth Saturday of the month at 9:30 AM). A guided tour is offered daily at 2 from the visitor center. Also be sure to visit the Bazaar del Mundo (*see #56*) for a sense of the region's Mexican heritage.

HEY, KIDS! When did they first start calling this area Old Town? In about 1868, when the building of "New Town" began, and the region's focus turned there. The new town area is now what's known as the Gaslamp Quarter in downtown San Diego.

KEEP IN MIND Younger kids seeking to blow off steam will enjoy the grass-filled Plaza, where they can run, play, and climb on the cannons (unarmed of course) while listening for mariachi music that often floats over from one of the many local Mexican restaurants. They'll also enjoy the Wells Fargo History Museum, where they can ogle (but not climb on) a real stagecoach, and the Seeley Stables, which has historic buggies and horse-drawn carriages; both are just off the Plaza.

PLAZA BONITA KIDS CLUB

Complete with a clown emcee, this mall-based interactive show tries hard to please a wide age range—and succeeds. Topping the program are participatory kid aerobics so your brood can get its wiggles out (and, in some cases, get primed for a nap). After that, different presentations each week might include a comedy-filled puppet show, a lively sing-along music program, or a visit with some exotic animals. The club also has theme shows—educational, but not dull—on such topics as water safety and the hazards of drugs.

Older toddlers, preschoolers, and younger elementary school–age kids should lap this up, and infants have been known to sit through most of the show, especially if music is on the program. Although kids up to age 12 are welcome to join the club, it may not

EATS FOR KIDS The food court on the second level has 11 eateries. Kids tend to like **Sbarro Pizza**, **Panda Express** (Chinese), or the corn dogs and fresh lemonade at **Hot Dog on a Stick**. There are also predictable favorites here, such as **Dairy Queen** and **McDonald's.**

KEEP IN MIND Obviously, part of the purpose of the Kids Club is to get you into the mall—and if you're a resident, at least once a week—but there are plenty of ways to amuse the kids here for an enjoyable afternoon without spending a bundle of money. Start by picking up one of the free "Kiddie Kruzzers" strollers that look like little red cars (at the information kiosk). Then take them to the "Playtown" area in the center, where they can frolic, slide, and play games (there are some coin-operated rides here). After that, head over to the carousel for a quick ride before the show starts.

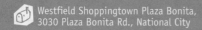

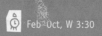

have as much appeal for those over age 9 or so—except for the big finish, when there's a prize drawing.

Free "membership" in the club includes registration for the shows and a ticket for the drawing, usually for a gift certificate or other item donated by a mall merchant. Members also receive discounts at vendors throughout the mall on the day of the show. Other Westfield Shoppingtown malls in the county offer similar clubs (at University Towne Center in La Jolla, Plaza Camino Real in Carlsbad, North County Fair in Escondido, and Parkway Plaza in El Cajon), so you can visit these when you are in a different part of town, or you can fill up your little one's week by going to all of them!

HEY, KIDS! The mall is as good a place as any to try out more of your Spanish (see #56 for more vocabulary), so here are a few starter phrases: *Habla ingles?* means Do you speak English? *Cuanto cuesta?* means How much does it cost? *Que hora es?* means What time is it? *Donde esta el bano?* means Where is the bathroom? Now, here's one to try out on your parents: *Por favor, dame* means Please give me—fill in the rest with your favorite: *un helado* (an ice cream), *unas dulces* (some candy), or *una galleta* (a cookie).

THE PRINCE AND THE PAUPER

Y ou'll find some old friends here, ones you can introduce to your kids. And with more than 75,000 books, these dear companions won't be too hard to find.

The fun at The Prince and the Pauper Collectible Children's Books is browsing the nooks and crannies of the 4,000-sq-ft store, as snaking bookcases reveal little corners perfect for tucking into a book. Most titles are gently used hardbacks. Some books are rare, many are collectible, and there are out-of-print, first edition, and signed volumes, too. This is why prices will range from a buck to thousands of bucks. The rarer and more valuable volumes are kept under glass, so there's no worry that your toddler will drool on a first edition.

The overhead signs indicate areas for each type of book—fairy tales or picture books, for instance—so it's easy to find your special interest. Along with old copies of such standbys as *Peter Pan* and *Alice in Wonderland*, entire cases are devoted to Mother Goose, mysteries, bedtime stories, and other genres, as well as groups of Golden Books and board books.

HEY, KIDS! Some of your favorite stories to read may actually be older than your parents (if you can believe it) and even your grandparents. Dr. Seuss's *Cat in the Hat*, a relative youngster, was first published in 1957. *Lord of the Rings* came out in 1953, and *Stuart Little* in 1945, and Winnie the Pooh first appeared in A.A. Milne's book *When We Were Very Young* in 1924. *Peter Pan* came out in 1904. *The Prince and the Pauper* (the story this shop is named for) was written by Mark Twain in 1882. And *Alice in Wonderland* was dreamt up by Lewis Carroll way back in the 1860s.

 3201 Adams Ave.

 Free

 M-Sa 10-6

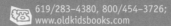 619/283-4380, 800/454-3726;
www.oldkidsbooks.com

 1 and up

There is also a section devoted to book series, such as Nancy Drew, Cherry Ames, the Hardy Boys, and the Bobbsey Twins. The Wizard of Oz books have their own special place of honor in a display near the front of the store. Contemporary titles, such as the popular (and hilarious—just ask a nearby fourth grader) Captain Underpants books, are also available.

When the littlest ones get tired of all that reading, they can talk to the green and yellow parrots that live here. They can then retire to their own castle, a sweet little play area with towers, a fantasy wall mural, and plenty of toys to keep them busy so that you can linger with your old friends for just a while longer.

EATS FOR KIDS
The **Antique Row Café** (3002 Adams Ave., 619/282-9750) has amazing breakfasts. Try **De-Mille's Italian Deli and Pizza Grotto** (3492 Adams Ave., 619/283-3153) or eat Mexican at **Villa del Mar** (3531 Adams Ave. #102, 619/563-9401). **Jyoti Bihanga** offers vegetarian cuisine, including "neatloaf" (3351 Adams Ave., 619/282-4116).

KEEP IN MIND The Prince and the Pauper is in the heart of the established community of Normal Heights. It's a great place to stroll and explore the antiques stores, other bookshops, restaurants, boutiques, and coffeehouses that line Adams Avenue. It's also home to Southern California's largest free music festival each September: the Adams Avenue Street Fair is a family-friendly event with more than 75 music performers and hundreds of vendors offering food, crafts, and rides. In April, a Roots Festival includes bluegrass, folk, and traditional music. Call 619/282-7329 for more information on both events.

QUAIL BOTANICAL GARDENS

They may grouse about coming here at first because of the name (it does sound a little too educational), so just bill it as a zoo, except with plants. And you won't be lying. Once your family gets here, they'll be enchanted by amazing, explorable landscapes. Your kids probably won't care that the bamboo grove in front of them is rare—their imaginations will already be working overtime as they imagine it as giant walls of some intriguing fortress. Likewise, the tremendous exotic trees and vines in the tropical areas may give them visions of being on a mysterious jungle quest. There will be new surprises at every turn as they chance upon a secluded waterfall, a stark desert panorama, and rain-forest wonders as they follow the garden pathways.

It's hard to believe that this all began as a private garden. Green thumbs Ruth and Charles Larabee bought the 30 acres for their private home, and donated it all to Encinitas in

EATS FOR KIDS The gift shop here sells some small snacks. Nearby is **Tomiko** (87 Encinitas Blvd., 760/633–3568) for Japanese specialties such as bento boxes and udon noodles. If you're in the mood for penne, ravioli, or other Italian dishes, try **Gusto Trattoria** (429 Encinitas Blvd., 760/436–8664).

KEEP IN MIND This property is vast, so if you don't think your kids will have the stamina to make it through the entire acreage, just hit some of the highlights, such as the desert and the walled and bamboo gardens, all just west and northwest of the entrance. If you're traveling with a more energetic group, also head northeast to the pantropical rain-forest display and the waterfall. Be sure to cross to the southern end of the parking lot to the Kumeyaay home site display to see a replica of a historic native people's village, surrounded by the California plants they used in their day-to-day lives.

230 Quail Gardens Dr., Encinitas

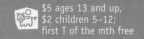 $5 ages 13 and up,
$2 children 5–12;
first T of the mth free

 Daily 9–5

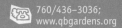 760/436–3036;
www.qbgardens.org

2 and up

1957. The gardens now serve as a plant conservation area and a preserve for historically significant plantings. There are more than 4,000 species of plants from 15 regions, further divided into habitats. The kids might particularly enjoy the alien-looking plants from the New and Old World deserts, such as the gargantuan-size cacti and the striking Dragon Tree that seeps bloodred sap.

You can explore the grounds on your own, or take the daily 10 AM tour. There's also a special children's tour offered on the first Tuesday of the month (admission is free that day, too) and construction is under way for a new children's garden area with specially designed interactive exhibits.

HEY, KIDS! Quail Gardens is named after the California quail, and you can see them here in the morning or late afternoon. Look for a bird that resembles a small chicken, with a black beak and gray, black, brown, and white feathers. You can tell it's a quail by the spray of black feathers that sticks up out of its head like a little poufed hat. This is the state bird of California, but it can also be found in parts of Oregon and Nevada.

REUBEN H. FLEET SCIENCE CENTER

 cience class was never this much fun. A visit here is more like going to a giant arcade, except each "game" actually demonstrates scientific principles, so the kids get to learn something from their play here. Just about everything is interactive, so the kids can touch, work, jiggle, wiggle, make faces, aim, and spin, all in the name of science.

Wear your running shoes, because kids tend to race among games. And be prepared for it to get pretty noisy in here, too. The five galleries are spread around two levels (with stair and elevator access), with exhibits covering technological innovations, satellite imaging, biology, space travel, and communications. Try to catch one of the live science demonstrations, held several times a day, at the Demonstration Station. Another treat is the ExploraZone, with 30 hands-on exhibits borrowed from San Francisco's famous Exploratorium.

Although the 2–6 set is free to explore the entire space, they get a dedicated place to experiment in the Little Learners Lab, where they can build with blocks, bang on bongos,

HEY, KIDS! Would you like to travel into space someday? If you are in the fifth grade or beyond, the Challenger Learning Center allows you or your parents the chance to simulate the experience of being an astronaut on a space station. You'll get to do experiments with realistic equipment, like check life support, monitor space experiments, launch a space probe, and analyze extraterrestrial samples. Missions include Return to the Moon, Rendezvous with a Comet, and Voyage to Mars. It's held on several Saturdays throughout the year, from 1 to 4 ($15 fee per person, reservations required).

1875 El Prado, Balboa Park

 619/238-1233; www.rhfleet.org

 Exhibits $6.75 ages 13 and up, $5 children 3–12, 1st T of mth free; exhibits and IMAX film $11.50 ages 13 and up, $8.50 kids 3–12; planetarium shows $6.75 ages 13 and up, $5.50 children 3–12

 M–Th 9:30–5, F and Sa 9:30–8, Su 9:30–6

 2 and up

and play with educational toys. Older kids will gravitate toward SciTours—a motion simulator ride that mimics a space trip—and the Virtual Zone, where they can wend their way through a meteor storm.

A big hit for nearly all kids is the IMAX theater (the only one in San Diego) with films on space travel, biology, animals, and extreme sports. The theater also has astronomy events such as the planetarium show and Star Party on the first Wednesday of the month at 7 PM. Family Science days on the third Saturday of each month, from 12 to 3, allow you and your children to work together on science experiments. Your greatest discovery after spending three to four hours here may be how easily you were able to give the kids an educational experience—and "scientifically" tire them out at the same time.

EATS FOR KIDS
Galileo's Café in the Science Center has sandwiches, salads, ice cream, pizza, snacks, and drinks. Or, stop on your way here at **La Salsa** (1010 University Ave., 619/543–0777) for grilled chicken or steak soft tacos that you can garnish at the fresh salsa bar.

KEEP IN MIND Balboa Park's Free Tuesdays program offers free admission to different museums on rotating Tuesdays throughout the month (permanent exhibits only, not to special shows or extras such as the IMAX). This is a great service, but it creates such crowds at the science center that you may want to visit on other days. If you do choose to come on Tuesday, arrive during lunchtime, or very late in the day.

ROHR PARK

Well loved and well used by the community, the 60 acres of mammoth Rohr Park cut a large swath of green between the communities of Chula Vista and Bonita in the south bay area of San Diego County. It's busy here every weekend (appreciably less crowded on weekdays) and you'll find the ever-present laughter infectious as you weave around the large picnic spreads, softball and basketball games, and kite flyers. Because of the park's size, you can avail yourself of all this activity and still carve out a private space for your family to enjoy the walking paths and gazebos, luscious trees, and endless grass.

A walking adventure will allow you and the kids to explore some of park's more unusual treasures. Hunt for "Fort Apache"—really a shaded picnic area and playground with swings, slide, and a climbing structure. If you trek to the northeastern end of the park, you might

EATS FOR KIDS There are several restaurants on nearby Bonita Road: **Buon Giorno** (4110 Bonita Rd., 619/475–2660) for Italian food, **House of Nine Dragons** (4164 Bonita Rd., 619/267–3200) for Chinese specialties, and the **Bonita Store** (4014 Bonita Rd., 619/479–3537) for Baja-style Mexican food.

GETTING THERE There are plenty of commercial services on the other side of the park, such as the restaurants listed here in EATS FOR KIDS. To get there, take Sweetwater Road west from the park (a left out of the parking lot). Turn left at Willow Road, then go left at Bonita Road. Or, go east on Sweetwater Road (turn right out of the lot). Make a right on Central, then turn right on Bonita Road. This will also put you on the path back toward I–805, and the Plaza Bonita Shopping Center is nearby, too (*see #29*).

catch some horses training in the equestrian ring. Dwellings worth spying are the Olde Adobe, an authentic 1800s home near the center of the park. Its rustic wood and clay architecture contrasts with the formality of nearby Rohr Manor, a redbrick and white wood house with an iron-railed second-floor balcony and distinct porthole windows, built here in 1938.

If you happen to visit on the second weekend of the month, the Chula Vista Live Steamers offer rides on a scaled-down steam locomotive from 12 to 3 (also on Labor Day weekend) and demonstrates model diesel and electric trains operating in the center of the park.

HEY, KIDS! The Olde Adobe building is about 200 years old, but it wasn't built in the park—it was moved here in 1938. The man who originally owned the land where Rohr Park is now was named Ruben Harrison. He liked to collect Native American artifacts and needed a place to keep them. When he found the Olde Adobe in the Cuyamaca Mountains, he had it taken apart piece by piece and brought down to his land here, where it was put back together again to house his collection.

SAN DIEGO AEROSPACE MUSEUM

I f it can fly, they probably have one here. This museum covers just about every mechanical flying machine from the time of Kitty Hawk to the space shuttle. Aircraft are everywhere: on the floor, hanging from the ceiling, and in displays, awesomely demonstrating America's aerospace history.

Preschoolers and young elementary school–age kids likely will want to "fly" through the place without stopping much, cruising through the exhibit rooms and ogling what's in the rafters. But if you have older kids with even the remotest interest in air or space travel, prepare to spend at least a couple of hours looking at displays, including replicas of the very first manned air-vehicle (a whimsical looking 1783 hot air balloon), the Wright Brothers' famous Flyer, and Lindbergh's *Spirit of St. Louis* (the original was built in San Diego).

In comparison with the 65 full-scale reproductions and original aircraft, there's also a collection of intricately constructed models—and their small size contrasts nicely with some of the

KEEP IN MIND If you're traveling with transportation junkies, take them to the next building north in Balboa Park to the San Diego Automotive Museum. The exhibits aren't as detailed as those at the Aerospace Museum, but there are more than 80 vintage vehicles to see, including horseless carriages, a Tin Lizzie (1924 Model T Ford), a Tucker Torpedo, a '57 Chevy, a rare 1966 Bizzarini, and a large collection of motorcycles—including something called a 1912 Flying Merkle. The museum is open daily 10–4:30 and costs $7 for ages 16 and up, $3 for children 3–15 (2080 Pan American Plaza, 619/231–2886).

2001 Pan American Plaza,
Balboa Park

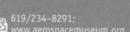
619/234-8291;
www.aerospacemuseum.org

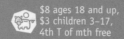
$8 ages 18 and up,
$3 children 3-17,
4th T of mth free

Daily 10-4:30 (closed holidays)

2 and up

larger craft in the Pavilion of Flight, such as the PBY-5A Catalina that soars overhead. You'll get to see some rare WWII fighters such as the British Spitfire, Japanese Zero, and U.S. Hellcat. There's also a Vietnam-era Huey Helicopter and one of only two Ryan X-13 Vertijets ever built. Don't miss the chance to take the kids to see astronaut spacesuits and a replica of an Apollo spacecraft. And when looking at the planes just isn't enough, your aviation fans will be able to climb into the pilot's seat of several aircraft in the You're a Pilot section, and can even try on a flight suit for size.

Also take a minute to point out the building's unique lifesaver-like shape to the kids. Although it's a fascinating piece of architecture, it can be tough on parents trying to keep track of small children, so try to keep them reined in here or you'll literally be running in circles after them.

EATS FOR KIDS
The spot closest to the museum in Balboa Park is the **Time-Out Café**, with sports star–theme sandwiches, in the San Diego Hall of Champions (see #22). A fun place to eat in nearby Hillcrest is the '50s–style **Corvette Diner** (3946 5th Ave., 619/542-1001) with burgers, shakes, and a real Corvette convertible.

HEY, KIDS! The museum keeps more of its airplanes at Gillespie Field (335 Kenney St., 619/234-8291), a small airport in El Cajon (about 10 mi east of Balboa Park). If you're lucky, you might also catch the staff restoring a plane or creating a replica. It's open to the public on Monday, Wednesday, and Friday from 8 to 3, and admission is free.

SAN DIEGO—CORONADO BAY FERRY

If you can use a fun, scenic, and inexpensive way to get the kids out on the water, San Diego's popular and perfect little solution is the 15-minute ferry ride between the city and Coronado. It leaves every hour on the hour from San Diego, and every hour on the half hour from Coronado.

Each end of the ferry's path also has handy attractions for kids. On the Coronado side, the Ferry Landing Marketplace, with its singular view of San Diego's skyline, is ideal for strolling, shopping, lunching, and even fishing. You can take bikes and strollers (no fee for the latter) aboard the ferry and then use them here on the winding waterfront paths, or you can rent bikes when you get to this side. There is a farmer's market held here

EATS FOR KIDS At the San Diego dock, get a burger at the **Bay Café** (1050 N. Harbor Dr., 619/595–1083). In Coronado at the Ferry Landing Marketplace (1201 First St. at B Ave.) there are many eateries, including **Deli By the Bay** (619/437–1006), with soups, salads, and sandwiches.

KEEP IN MIND You can take a longer boat trip with a tour of the bay on one of the San Diego Harbor Excursion Tours that leave from the same dock as the ferry. They have 1-hr and 2½-hr narrated tours that cruise around the bay, focusing on landmarks and ships in port. There are also special dinner cruises nightly. From December through March, whale-watching excursions take you out to sea for a close-up look at migrating California gray whales. For information and prices call 800/442–7847.

Broadway Pier at 1050 N. Harbor Dr.
(San Diego side); Ferry Landing at 1201
First St. at B Ave. (Coronado side)

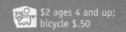 $2 ages 4 and up;
bicycle $.50

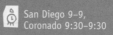 San Diego 9–9,
Coronado 9:30–9:30

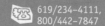 619/234-4111,
800/442-7847

 All ages

every Tuesday from 2:30 to 6. If you're lucky, you'll be there on a day when the offerings include baked cookies and fresh tomato salsa and tortilla chips.

Back across the bay on the San Diego side, you can walk along the Embarcadero, where the *Berkeley* and the *Star of India,* highlights of the Maritime Museum (*see #20*) are moored. The path here is wide and stroller friendly, although you have to watch smaller children extra carefully near the edge of the water, as there is a sharp drop. You can also head south past Tuna Harbor on a leisurely mile-long walk to Seaport Village (*see #12*), where a ride on the Broadway Flying Horses Carousel might be in order.

HEY, KIDS! Guess what? Although it is known as Coronado Island, Coronado is not really an island . . . it's a peninsula. That means it's connected by land, in this case a thin strip of beach on the southern end known as the Silver Strand, and is accessible by car from the south bay area. But even with the existence of the Coronado Bridge, built in 1969, driving between San Diego and Coronado is not as convenient, or ever as much fun, as riding the ferry.

SAN DIEGO HALL OF CHAMPIONS

As one of the only museums in the country with a multisport emphasis, there's plenty here for sports fans to cheer about. Baseball enthusiasts can take a gander at memorabilia from the late, great Ted Williams, including his two MVP awards and his Presidential Medal of Freedom. Motor-sports fans will get to see two actual midget racing cars, along with an exhibit on auto racing from 1907 to the present. And in the media center, you can watch some of your favorite plays again, beaming from a bank of 16 video screens. You and your kids can also try your hand (or voice) at calling the play-by-play of a videotaped game (and your efforts will be replayed, so you can check out your performance).

As with all the displays here, there's a broad focus on local sports, from Little League through the pros. The football area includes an extensive history of the Chargers since 1960, and you'll get to see their 1963 AFL championship trophy. The museum also has

HEY, KIDS! Going to a game while you're in town? Here's a handy list of our local teams: the NFL team is the Chargers, the Major League Baseball team is the Padres, the NHL team is the Gulls, and the Women's United Soccer Association team is the Spirit. The college teams are the San Diego State University Aztecs, the University of San Diego Toreros, and the University of California–San Diego Titans. If you're an Olympic sports fan, you can check out where many summer athletes train at the ARCO U.S. Olympic Training Center (see #60).

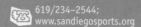

temporary exhibitions that zero in on sports history and culture, which might interest visitors who are not passionate spectators. In the past, exhibits have explored the 1936 Berlin Games in "The Nazi Olympics," an exhibit produced by the United States Holocaust Museum. The museum has also taken up the future of sports, with shows on popular youth activities such as skateboarding, surfing, and street luge.

The highest sports honor in the city is to be inducted into the Breitbard Hall of Fame, which pays tribute to athletes who were either from San Diego or played here. Among our local heroes are football's Dan Fouts, Fred Dryer, and Marcus Allen, basketball's Bill Walton, baseball's Dave Winfield, Tony Gwynn, and Rollie Fingers, boxing's Ken Norton, and skateboarding's Tony Hawk (*see #35* for more on Tony's influence on San Diego).

EATS FOR KIDS

Inside the museum is a deli-style restaurant, the **Time-Out Café.** Here, your kids can pick a sandwich named after their favorite athlete, such as Archie Moore Ham and Swiss and the Marcus Allen Hot Dog. You can also stop in nearby Hillcrest on your way here to do some carbo-loading at **Bronx Pizza** (111 Washington St., 619/291–3341).

KEEP IN MIND If your kids are revved up to polish some of their own sports abilities, the Morley Field Sports Complex in the northeastern corner of Balboa Park has venues for tennis, softball, baseball, soccer, rugby, football, shuffleboard, and basketball. The indoor/outdoor complex also has a swimming pool, a fitness course, a bicycle velodrome, an archery range, bocce courts, a Frisbee golf course, bicycle paths, picnic areas, and a tot lot, so even the littlest ones can play (2221 Morley Dr., 619/692–4919).

SAN DIEGO JUNIOR THEATRE

This is, quite simply, a theater for kids and starring kids. These family-friendly productions will not only get your children excited about the stage, but might also inspire them to do a little acting, singing, and dancing themselves.

Junior Theatre produces six stage plays and musicals each year, and every one has a cast culled from students of their extensive theater arts program, which offers more than 200 classes in acting, singing, dancing, voice, and other areas. Classes are generally held (at 1650 El Prado) in the late afternoon and on weekends, and draw kids ranging in age from 8 to 18 from all over the county. The theater presents both classics and newer works, such as *Cinderella, You're a Good Man, Charlie Brown, The Miracle Worker,* and *How to Eat Like a Child.*

In the same way that kids like to watch movies starring children, they're similarly drawn in by children in stage performances, and that's what makes this experience so special.

EATS FOR KIDS The **Village Grill** (Village Pl. and Old Globe Way), just north of the theater in Balboa Park, is a good stop for burgers and fries. On the way to the show, stop by for pizza on the patio at **Sanfillippo Restaurant** (3515 5th Ave., 619/299–6080).

KEEP IN MIND Take your little theater fans down to the western end of Balboa Park to see the Old Globe Theatre complex. There are three theaters here, and one is a re-creation of the Bard's playhouse in London. Many productions are performed here throughout the year (some are kid friendly), and two Shakespearean plays are offered each summer. They also have backstage tours on weekend mornings. A relatively new San Diego holiday tradition is the Globe's production of *How the Grinch Stole Christmas* (call for tickets now, because they sell out very early—619/239–2255).

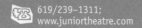

Casa del Prado Theatre, Balboa Park

$7–$10 adults, $5–$8 children; class prices vary

F 7, Sa–Su 2; class times vary

619/239–1311;
www.juniortheatre.com

3 and up

The plays here tend to hold the young audience members' attention in a way that conventional theater productions cannot. Also, the Casa del Prado Theatre is not overwhelming, even with 650 seats, so it's easy for kids to see and hear the action onstage.

Established in 1948 as a children's theater wing of the Old Globe Theatre (just west of here in Balboa Park), the Junior Theatre is now an independent, nonprofit organization. San Diego has an active and ample theater community for these kids to break into— there are about 50 theater groups and venues here, including the renowned La Jolla Playhouse. They might even achieve fame beyond the borders of the city, like Junior Theatre alumni Brian Stokes Mitchell, Annette Bening, Dennis Hopper, and Raquel Welch.

HEY, KIDS! You may love the theater, but maybe going up on stage is not your thing. Hey, no problem! Besides actors, singers, and dancers, there are many, many people working behind the scenes, including the director, choreographer, makeup people, and various engineers. A critical behind-the-scenes job belongs to the stage manager, who serves as a go-between for the director and cast and the crew of the production, and is also responsible for all the on-stage and backstage events (with the help of stagehands, who are often stage managers in training).

SAN DIEGO MARITIME MUSEUM

This is more like visiting Captain Hook's ship than a museum. Floating on the waterfront near downtown San Diego, the Maritime Museum is made up entirely of ships that you can explore from bow to stern. Admission gets you on board the 1863 sailing ship *Star of India*, the 1898 steam ferryboat *Berkeley*, and the 1904 steam yacht *Medea*.

With tall sails and a main mast that soars 124 feet into the air, the *Star of India* is the world's oldest working sailing ship (it sails about once a year). Kids can stand in front of the ship's wheel, look out over the ocean, feel the sway of the waves, and get a sense of what traveling may have been like on board this ship during one of its 21 circumnavigations. Preschoolers and elementary-age kids like the fact that they can climb up and down narrow stairs, peek out of portholes, explore each deck, and touch most parts of the ship.

Have a look in the upper-deck passenger rooms. Although the size of a cramped walk-in closet, this was luxurious compared with how most emigrants had to travel on the 'tween

KEEP IN MIND Look out for special events at the museum: in summer, there's Movies before the Mast, where a film is projected onto a sail on the *Star of India*. See pirate reenactments and lots of singing during the Sea Chantey Festival each July. The best of *Pirates of Penzance* and *HMS Pinafore* are occasionally staged on board. In September, there is the Festival of the Sail, when other tall ships come into the bay, and the *Star of India* leads them out to sea in a kind of water parade. Most events do not require reservations, but call the museum for details. While you're in this area, also consider a walk to Seaport Village (see #12) or a ride on the San Diego–Coronado Bay Ferry (see #23).

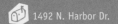 1492 N. Harbor Dr.

 619/234-9153;
www.sdmaritime.org

 $6 ages 18 and up,
$4 youths 13–17,
$3 children 6–12

 Daily 9–8

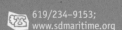 2 and up

deck; go downstairs and imagine living in this damp, dark area during a four-month voyage with 400 other people!

Most of the museum's exhibits are on the middle deck of the *Berkeley,* and you can pretty much breeze right through these (they cover nautical history). But school-age kids will want to linger over the collection of ship models. Be sure to go downstairs to the boiler room. Older kids will like the fact that it's a little scary down here—it's close, musty, and built of industrial metal, quite a contrast from the genteel upper decks made of wood and windows, where passengers strolled, chatted, and dined when the *Berkeley* ferried them across San Francisco Bay for 60 years.

EATS FOR KIDS
Just south of here is **Anthony's Fish Grotto** (1360 N. Harbor Dr., 619/232–5103), good for a hearty seafood meal; for a quick meal or snack, try their **Fishette** next door (619/232–5105). For burgers, go across the street to the **Elephant & Castle Pub & Restaurant** (1355 N. Harbor Dr., 619/234–9977).

HEY, KIDS! The *Star of India* has earned the right to spend her retirement years floating leisurely here in San Diego harbor, because she survived a lot of disasters that other ships did not. Named the *Euterpe* when she first sailed from the Isle of Man in 1863, she made it through a cyclone, recovered from many collisions, sailed through severe storms, dodged icebergs, and was frozen in place several times while working the salmon fisheries in Alaska between 1902 and 1923. When purchased by Americans in 1906, she was renamed in honor of her early voyages to India.

SAN DIEGO MODEL RAILROAD MUSEUM

If your kids like trains, they'll be in choo-choo heaven here. The place is jammed with tiny trains running on tracks through amazingly detailed lilliputian landscapes with miniature people and animals, houses, office buildings, farms, and even swimming pools.

It could take days to visit all of the regions of San Diego, but in a single trip here you'll see many of them, minuscule representations of the railroad corridors that run through Rose Canyon, Union Station, the airport, downtown, National City, Lemon Grove, La Mesa, Santee, and El Cajon. Elevated ramps allow you to get a gargantuan view of these little worlds and the trains that run continuously through them.

At 24,000 sq ft, this museum has the largest indoor railroad display in the world. Since it opened in 1982, it has relied on the work of volunteer members of local train clubs, who

EATS FOR KIDS Inside the Casa de Balboa Building is the **Café in the Park,** where you can get muffins, sandwiches, salads, and beverages (619/237–0322). There are also many food kiosks along the Prado outside the building that sell hot dogs, ice cream, snacks, and drinks.

HEY, KIDS! Getting close to a moving train is an age-old dare among kids, but know that this is also an age-old problem: Operation Lifesaver is an organization that gives out information on the importance of train safety, and here are some things they want you to bear in mind when you're near a train track: expect a train to come at any time, never drive around crossing gates, watch for a second train, never race a train, and remember that trains can't stop quickly.

1649 El Prado, Casa de Balboa,
Balboa Park

$4 ages 16 and up,
children 15 and under
free with adult; 1st
T of mth free

T–F 11–4, Sa–Su 11–5,
closed holidays

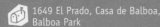
619/696-0199;
www.sdmodelrailroadm.com

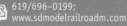
2 and up

create displays and repair and maintain the trains and vignettes. Their exhibits represent California's railroad lines in diminutive proportions: the Cabrillo and Southwestern is an O scale line ($\frac{1}{48}$ size), the San Diego and Arizona Eastern is an HO scale line ($\frac{1}{87}$ size), and the teensy Pacific Desert line is N scale ($\frac{1}{160}$ size!).

Of course, after seeing enough of these trains, your aspiring conductors and engineers will be itching to move some locomotives, and they can, at the Lionel Interactive Train exhibit, where kids get to control the switches for model trains that run along three different layouts (and friendly engineers are available to help out and answer questions). There are also other amusements in here, such as a wooden train set for toddler play, and train-theme videos and computer games.

KEEP IN MIND If the kids would like to get a behind-the-scenes look at how the models and landscapes are put together, bring them here on Tuesday and Friday nights and watch the club volunteers do construction. Please enter through the back door. For more information call the La Mesa Model Railroad Club (619/696-0199) or the San Diego Society of N-Scale (619/669-1521). There are also special family days one Sunday a month with workshops, crafts, and historical reenactments. And in the summertime, day camps for kids are filled with train-related activities.

SAN DIEGO MUSEUM OF ART

18

"S weetie," you'll say to Junior, "note the artist's remarkable use of light in this portrait, *Infante don Felipe*. It was painted way back in 1580. Junior? Come back here!"

Okay, so *you* might care that many of the greats—Rembrandt, Degas, Monet, Matisse, Dali, Picasso, Goya, and El Greco—are represented here, and if you're lucky you'll be able to soak up a few of them. But unless you're with a serious young art student, it's probably best to whisk through these galleries with the kids and head for the art that's more accessible to them. This might include the contemporary art, with familiar images and bright colors, or the extensive collection of exotic Asian art that includes depictions of animals, dragons, and supernatural beings.

What really wows the kids here is the eclectic mix of changing exhibits with themes as varied as atomic age design, Degas sculptures, Mexican treasures, and "Star Wars: The Magic

KEEP IN MIND Don't miss some of the other great art in Balboa Park. The world folk art at Mingei International Museum (1439 El Prado, 619/239–0003) includes dolls and toys. Young shutterbugs can see how artists capture the world through the lens of a camera at the Museum of Photographic Arts (1649 El Prado, 619/238–7559). There is always something interesting to see at the Centro Cultural de la Raza (2125 Park Blvd., 619/235–6135), starting on the outside with a colorful mural on the circular-shape building, and continuing inside with the exhibits on the art of Mexicans, Chicanos, and other indigenous people of the region.

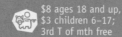
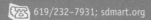
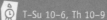

of the Myth." The museum's goal is to "connect people to art and art to people," so they work to present exhibits with broad appeal, focusing on a good mix of American work, international treasures, and shows with recognized masters. A schedule of lectures, concerts, and movies rounds out the offerings.

The museum spices things up with free Family Festivals, where you and your children are invited to join in hands-on art making, see artist demonstrations, go on special tours, or watch live musical entertainment. And since most kids would rather make art than look at it, the Museum Art School runs studio and gallery classes for children ages 4–18. Summertime day camps also have courses in animal drawing, filmmaking, and cartooning (call for class fees).

HEY, KIDS! You'll find paintings here by the famous Spanish artist El Greco, though he wasn't Spanish and that wasn't his real name. Born in Greece in 1541, El Greco (Spanish for "the Greek") didn't move to Spain until 1577—and his true name was Domenikos Theotokopoulos.

EATS FOR KIDS Continue your art tour at **The Prado** (1549 El Prado, 619/557–9441), brimming with colorful glass artwork. It's the only true full-service restaurant in Balboa Park, serving salads, pastas, seafood, sandwiches, and tapas. If you want to venture to some of the nearby neighborhoods, have lunch in University Heights at **Mama's Bakery and Lebanese Deli** (4237 Alabama St., 619/688–0717) for chicken, rice, and fresh pita bread combinations. For those picky eaters, there are many PB&J choices downtown at **Nutter's** (428 C St., Ste. 101, 619/239–7075).

SAN DIEGO MUSEUM OF MAN

The next time you call your kids "little monkeys," you can bring them here to prove that you weren't entirely kidding. One of the big draws is "Footsteps through Time— Four Million Years of Evolution," where you can see more than 100 re-creations of early humans, primates, and even future "cyborgs" (part human and part machine). It might amuse your kids to learn, for instance, that if evolution had taken a slightly different path, they might be walking around today with a prehensile tail.

After this walk down monkey lane, you can move on to other areas of the museum. Particularly worthy are exhibits on the Kumeyaay—the native people who inhabited the San Diego region—and other indigenous peoples of the Southwest, with examples of their handmade tools, textiles, pottery, and baskets. On weekdays, you can also watch tortillas being made in the traditional manner (and even purchase a fresh, warm example for a

HEY, KIDS!
Many scientists believe that the closest evolutionary relatives to humans are the common chimpanzee and the Bonobo (also known as the pygmy chimp), perhaps because there's only a .027% molecular genetic difference between us and them!

KEEP IN MIND Watch out for the mummies here when touring the museum with the squeamish or nightmare prone—in general, with kids 8 and younger. The Egyptian mummy is, thankfully, wrapped. But the others here are not, and they are pretty gruesome to the eye. And you will probably want to bypass the museum's exhibit of Inquisition torture implements (the kindly staff members at the entrance will likely warn you about this when they see you coming in with young children).

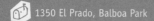 1350 El Prado, Balboa Park

 $6 ages 18 and up,
$3 children 6–17;
3rd T of mth free

 Daily 10–4:30

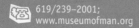 619/239–2001;
www.museumofman.org

 3 and up

snack). An exhibit on ancient Egypt includes 3,000-year-old artifacts such as masks, amulets, shrines, falcons, and a real mummy. There are some North and South American mummies displayed in this area, too (the yuck factor of this alone makes the trip worthwhile for older kids).

The younger set can dress up like Egyptians in the Children's Discovery Center, where they can also play with reproductions of ancient Egyptian artifacts, sit on a throne, pretend to travel on a boat down the Nile, hang out in an 18th-dynasty noble's home, try out a woven bed, check out an archaeological site, decode some hieroglyphics, and start their own dynasty by building a pyramid out of blocks. The museum also has many educational programs, such as summer day camps, where the kids can learn more about mummies, art, forensics, and anthropology.

EATS FOR KIDS On the weekends only, you can lunch at **Lady Carolyn's Pub** (619/231–1941 Ext. 2751), an outdoor eatery in the Old Globe Theatre's complex next door. They serve sandwiches, soups, and salads. Gazing at handmade objects may put you in the mood for handmade bread, and the best in the city is not too far from here at **Bread and Cie** (350 University Ave., 619/683–9322). Their freshly baked breads include kalamata olive, sourdough, and rosemary with olive oil. They also make sandwiches with them that you can eat here or take out for a picnic.

SAN DIEGO NATURAL HISTORY MUSEUM

Dinosaurs, insects, and snakes—oh, my! If your kids are into creatures, be they furry, scaly, feathery, or even extinct, they'll have a ball here. The exhibits tend to focus on things that kids can get excited about, such as fossils, sharks, bears, and crocodiles.

The museum works to incorporate touchable, interactive displays into their collections. Popular exhibits include nearly life-size, robotic moving (and sound-making) dinosaurs, a must-see that's typically available every couple of years (kids 5 and up won't find it too scary). Other exhibits have real specimens (there are more than 7.5 million fossils and specimens from air, land, and sea here), some stuffed, and some very much animated, like the live and crawling (in appropriate enclosures) black, white, and red striped California mountain king snake. You'll have to look a little more closely to see the speckled rattlesnake and western banded gecko, as their camouflage-like skins make them nearly invisible to

KEEP IN MIND There are many fun educational programs sponsored by the museum, such as overnight trips (to see cave paintings in Baja), children's classes (such as photo safaris), family programs (such as kayaking and fossil digs), free guided nature walks (held throughout the county), day camps, lectures, and films. Each weekend you can bring the kids to Wacky Science Sundays with Ms. Frizzle (of Scholastic's Magic School Bus) to see a live performance (hourly from 11:30 to 3:30). And on the first Saturday of each month you can join in special fun activities at Family Days from 11 to 3.

 1788 El Prado, Balboa Park

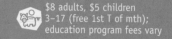 $8 adults, $5 children
3–17 (free 1st T of mth);
education program fees vary

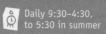 Daily 9:30–4:30,
to 5:30 in summer

 619/232-3821;
www.sdnhm.org

 All ages

the eye in their natural environments. There are other creepy-crawlies to take a gander at, too, such as furry-legged spiders, frighteningly huge cockroaches, and fuzzy red and black velvet ants.

In Balboa Park since 1933, the museum has been undergoing an expansion plan that will ultimately double the size of the building. In the meantime, you'll still be able to peruse fossils found right here in San Diego County—including humongous whale bones, frighteningly sharp-tooth shark jaws, and some much older pieces, such as the tusk from a real mastodon that was dug up in nearby National City—it dates to the Pleistocene era (10,000–1.8 million years ago). There are ancient mollusk shells here that were discovered nearby in 1998 during construction at the San Diego Hall of Champions (see #22). This of course means that 2–3 million years ago, the entire park area was under the ocean!

HEY, KIDS! Since they've collected more than 5 million marine specimens at the museum, it's a good source of information on where to go to collect seashells. Although you can pick up empty shells at most beaches, the museum recommends going to Tourmaline Beach in the Pacific Beach area.

EATS FOR KIDS For a further appreciation of nature, take the kids to the Japanese Friendship Garden, also in Balboa Park (near the Organ Pavilion). Here you can enjoy a lunch or snack of sushi, noodles, rice, soup, salad, and tea at the **Tea Pavilion** (619/231–0470), which has a courtyard and a deck with a view of the garden. For family-style Italian food and plenty of kitsch, head to nearby downtown San Diego to **Buca di Beppo** (705 6th Ave., 619/233–PAPA), where the servings are ample enough to feed a dinosaur.

SAN DIEGO WILD ANIMAL PARK

Go ahead. Tell the kids that you're taking them on a safari into the heart of Africa. Okay, so it's only a re-creation of the African landscape, but it has nearly everything you would find there—cheetahs, gazelles, okapi, and monkeys—and a few things that are harder to get on a real safari, like pizza.

The Heart of Africa is just one of the attractions at the Wild Animal Park, a sister site to the San Diego Zoo (*see #14*). On a staggering 1,800 acres, this natural environment gives animals the space to "herd and flock together, migrate, forage and breed." They run freely through the savannah-like landscapes, climbing rocky ridges and lapping water at tranquil pools. From many viewing areas you'll see wide green vistas of undulating, tree-filled land nestled within a ring of bordering hillsides. The park helps further the delicious illusion that you're trekking through the wild by placing more conventional animal enclosures (like for lowland gorillas) and service areas for dining and shopping in an African village–like setting that surrounds the Mombassa Lagoon.

HEY, KIDS!
Are you wondering why they're called white rhinos when they look brownish-gray? Do they just need a bath? It traces back to a word the Boers used to describe the rhinos's wide upper lip—"wide" was translated incorrectly as "white," and the name stuck!

KEEP IN MIND It not only looks like Africa here, but sometimes feels like it, too, as Escondido (35 mi northeast of San Diego) can get very hot in summer and early fall, so come in the morning. Early birds can enjoy the Sunrise Safari in August, when the park opens at 7:30. Or, beat the heat by going late to "The Park at Dark," in the summer when the park is open until 10. For an extra special experience, sign up for the Roar and Snore Camp-Over, where you, the kids, and the animals have a slumber party.

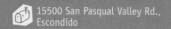 15500 San Pasqual Valley Rd., Escondido

 706/747-8702, 619/234-6541; www.wildanimalpark.org

 $26.50 ages 12 and up, $19.50 children 3–11; two-park ticket (Zoo and Wild Animal Park) $46.80 ages 12 and up, $31.40 children 3–11; parking $6

 Daily 9–4 (grounds close at 5); hrs vary seasonally

 1 and up

You can see most of the park on the Wgasa Bush Line Railway, a 65-minute narrated tour that passes through the physical center of the park to see rhinos, antelopes, and other creatures. The railway is suitable for school-age kids on up, but toddlers and preschoolers might get too squirmy, especially after what will be a long wait in line for the tram. The younger set will cotton more to Nairobi Village, where they can jump on giant lily pads and crawl inside an aardwolf den, and befriend deer, sheep, and goats at the Petting Kraal. Good for all ages is Condor Ridge, where a 430-ft-long trail leads to a viewing area for this huge and very rare bird—there are only about 150 of them left in the world. Have a stroller on hand for this and the Heart of Africa, and be sure to bring along hats, water, and sunscreen for all—remember, it's a jungle out there.

EATS FOR KIDS   If you travel into the Heart of Africa, be sure to stop for a bite at the **Okavango Outpost**, where the outside patio has a spectacular view. Near the Wgasa Bush Line Station is the **Thorn Tree Terrace** for burgers, sandwiches, and salads. For Italian and Asian specialties, try the **Mombasa Island Cooker** (they also have salads and burgers). They don't have straws or drink lids here (they could endanger the animals), so bring along your own lidded and sippy cups so you can split up drinks and keep the kids hydrated.

SAN DIEGO ZOO

Wouldn't it be great to visit with gorillas in an African rain forest one moment, then be transported the next to an arctic tundra to watch polar bears frolic in icy water? You can accomplish this feat without superpowers—just visit this zoo, "world-famous" for its awesome and rare animals from around the globe, and, no doubt, one of the main reasons you came to San Diego. You will not be disappointed.

Amazing enough is that this 100-acre oasis, composed of canyons and mesas, exotic plant life, and more than 4,000 animals, is smack in the middle of the city, just blocks up the hill from downtown San Diego in Balboa Park. In contrast to its sister Wild Animal Park (*see #15*), which at 1,800 acres screams big, the zoo feels expansive and cozy at once, tempting you to walk much of it. Still, you might want to begin with a leisurely overview: the 40-minute guided bus tour covers a lot of ground, allowing your brood to pick out animals they want to see in more detail. You can also get on and off an express bus that

KEEP IN MIND Want a great day at the zoo? Just arrive early, plan out your routes, and be sun smart. The animals are most active and vocal in the morning. The grounds are stroller friendly, but some inclines are very steep, so check with the information desk for the gentlest routes. The best way to cross the zoo quickly is on the Skyfari aerial tram (plus the kids love riding above the trees). You will be out in the sun most of the day at the zoo, so to avoid crisping your little critters, remember these three words: sunscreen, hats, water.

2920 Zoo Dr., in Balboa Park

 619/234-3153; sandiegozoo.org

 $19.50 ages 12 and up, $11.75 children ages 3–11; two-park ticket (Zoo and Wild Animal Park) $46.80 ages 12 and up, $31.40 children 3–11; bus tour and Skyfari ride extra

 Daily 9–4 (grounds close at 5); hrs vary seasonally

All ages

circulates around the zoo. While on foot, don't-miss natural habitats include Tiger River, Ituri Forest, and Gorilla Tropics—each so realistically appointed with native plants and authentic sounds and scents that you might forget you're not on safari.

Of course, pay your respects to pandas Shi Shi, Bai Yun, and Hua Mei, the zoo's de facto mascots and major draw; watching them gnaw on bamboo, lumber around, and nudge each other is a sweet memory to savor. Preschoolers particularly like the animal shows and the children's zoo, with its smaller enclosures. The petting area is benign enough, but be prepared for it to either enchant or startle your littlest ones, as tots react differently to the roaming and curious goats and sheep. Before leaving the zoo, take a peek into the nursery where the newborn animals are cared for—it will drive home what a nurturing and special place the zoo truly is.

HEY, KIDS! The zoo works hard to help protect endangered animals—some are almost extinct. You too can help preserve the natural habitats of the pandas, black rhinos, cheetahs, and other creatures by recycling your trash. To this end, the zoo's concessions don't give you drinking straws or lids, which can end up inside the enclosures and harm creatures determined to snack on them. And under no circumstances feed the animals!

SANTEE DRIVE-IN

S oon they may go the way of the silent pictures, but a few honest-to-goodness drive-ins still stubbornly endure. Thousands of these theaters dotted the country in the late 1960s—California alone had around 250—but now the state is down to around two dozen, and they're dwindling fast. What's especially scrappy about this one is that it's been unpretentiously plugging along uninterrupted and virtually unchanged since it opened in 1958.

There are two screens now instead of one, but otherwise, the landscape here is vintage drive-in, with vast areas of asphalt unfolding in front of each large white screen, with a building in the middle of the property serving as snack bar/projection booth/rest-room area. A double feature is part of the deal, so plan on a late night; programs change weekly (usually with at least one family-friendly option) and play year-round. The shows begin at dusk, and the first movie plays again after the second, should you need to catch it again after certain members of your party pass out.

GETTING THERE The drive-in is on the eastern edge of Santee, almost to Lakeside. Take Mission Gorge Road all of the way east through Santee, until the road turns into Woodside, where you'll continue east. The drive-in is on the north side.

EATS FOR KIDS The snack bar has typical offerings: popcorn, soda, candy, and sometimes pizza, hot dogs, and nachos. For a meal before the movies, stop by **Magnolia Mulvaneys** (8861 N. Magnolia Ave., 619/448–8550) with kids' meals including a shrimp boat and chicken strips. About half a mile southwest of the drive-in is **The Valley House** (10767 Woodside Ave., 619/562–7878), where you can get one of their special Iowa Porker sandwiches (pork tenderloin) and other hearty entrees. A local favorite is **Panda Country** (9621 Mission Gorge Rd., 619/449–7061) for Chinese food, especially the many combo plates.

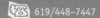 10990 N. Woodside Ave., Santee

 $6 adults,
$3 children

 M–Th opens 7:30, F and Sa 8

619/448–7447

All ages

One thing that is different about Santee and other drive-ins is that people don't always stay in their cars. Many people sit on lawn chairs or back up their trucks and vans to face the screen so kids can snuggle up inside and watch the movie. Nowadays, you listen to the movie through your car radio (they'll give you the station number) so you can hear it from the collective vehicles when outside, but you'll hear the dialogue a little better if you do it the old-fashioned way and sit inside your car.

A big advantage here is that unlike a conventional theater, you can walk your kids around if they get restless, all without missing the movie or getting disapproving looks. You're free to bring your own munchies, but for the sake of tradition have the kids make the trip here in their pajamas and slippers (as you may have once done) to buy some popcorn.

KEEP IN MIND Santee is about 17 mi east of San Diego. If you make the trip out this way, you can stop and spend the afternoon at Santee Lakes (9040 Carlton Oaks Dr. 619/596–3141). There are seven small lakes here to explore on 190 acres. The kids can fish, picnic, hike, and go to the playground. You can also rent boats and aqua cycles. The park is open daily Monday–Thursday 8 to sunset, and Friday–Sunday 6 to sunset ($2–$3 entrance fee per car). If you're so inclined, you can also camp here overnight.

SEAPORT VILLAGE

Waterfront complex Seaport Village has a bona-fide gem: the Broadway Flying Horses Carousel. Its vibrantly painted animals have been refurbished to their 1890 splendor, and kids can pick from enchanting horses, dogs, and even goats for a buck a ride. Visiting this magical merry-go-round, as well as the chance to stroll along prime bayside property, makes a trip to Seaport Village worthwhile—despite its possible retail dangers.

The 14-acre "village" was styled after California's historic, turn-of-the-century seaports, so its three plazas of shops and restaurants look like old Monterey, San Francisco, and Mexico, respectively. It's a pleasant place to shop, with a smattering of toy and game stores to keep your young browsers happy, as well as some eclectic places selling such wares as electric toothbrush holders or left-handed oven mitts. Many of these shops might be more pleasurable with kids 5 and up, as several stores have breakables and are not all that stroller

EATS FOR KIDS Near the carousel is a bevy of kid-friendly, take-out type restaurants with outdoor tables. Choose from fish-and-chips at **Marion's Fish Market,** hot dogs at **Seaport Grill,** pizza at **Assagio,** or the **San Diego Burger Company.** If you want a restaurant meal with a view of the water, try **Edgewater Grill** for pizza, pasta, and steak, or the **San Diego Pier Café** for fresh seafood. You can get snacks at **Seaport Village Popcorn Co.,** **Ben and Jerry's Ice Cream,** or the **Seaport Coffee and Fudge Factory.**

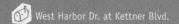

friendly. Know that the village is a worthy stop even if you avoid the shops altogether; if that's your strategy, as you leave the carousel (it's near the west plaza parking lot), head toward the water and walk southeast along the boardwalk that edges the bay. The walkway is wide and stroller friendly, and you can gaze at the boats as you meander toward Embarcadero Marina Park North, where the kids can run on the grass and climb trees.

For a nice outing, come ride the carousel and have lunch (eat at one of the outdoor restaurants or picnic at the park). There are also many free music performances, with genres as varied as jazz, blues, and kazoo. You do have to pay for parking, but they validate with a purchase, so you may want to scurry into at least one store before buying your carousel tickets.

HEY, KIDS! Although they don't look it, the carousel's animals are more than 100 years old. Charles Loof hand-carved them way back in 1890. The carousel started out at Coney Island in New York and came to Seaport Village in 1980.

KEEP IN MIND If you come here with school-age kids, steer clear of the arcade, or your entire afternoon will be lost (along with much of your cash). It is challenging to avoid since it's near the carousel, so you might have to, well, dissemble with an explanation such as, "Gosh, too bad they're having a private birthday party there today—maybe next time." If this doesn't work, just high-tail it out of there with a promise to visit the nearby Maritime Museum (see #20) or take a ferry ride (see #23).

SEAWORLD SAN DIEGO

Is this an aquarium or a theme park? It's both—you will get to feed dolphins and walk through a tunnel brimming with sharks, but there are rides and animal shows here, too. You'll be shelling out a steep admission fee, but you'll be getting a full day of not-so-standard theme park activities that are actually good for the brain.

Upon entering the 189-acre park, you'll get a map listing show times for such big draws as the Shamu Adventure and Dolphin Discovery. Once you nail down which shows you're catching, decide which habitats and other attractions you want to fit in between them.

School-age kids will like Shipwreck Rapids, a water raft ride that will leave them soaked, as well as the Sky Tower Ride, which takes you 320 ft into the air for a spectacular view of the park and adjacent Mission Bay (for an additional charge). Preschoolers enjoy the

HEY, KIDS!
Those killer whales you see at the Shamu Adventure aren't really whales. They're actually the largest members of the dolphin family. *Ornicus Orca* (their name in Latin) are very intelligent animals that travel in packs (like wolves) and communicate with each other through sounds.

EATS FOR KIDS At **Shipwreck Reef Café** you can get dinner and a show. This cafeteria-style restaurant has a variety of hot entrees, salads, and desserts—and has stages sprinkled throughout its patio area where trainers visit with animals such as otters, sea lions, penguins, and birds (it's very busy here right after the Shamu Adventure show lets out, so just don't come here then). There are many other food and snack kiosks throughout the park. Or, sit down for spaghetti and salad at **Mama Stella's Italian Kitchen** near the park's entrance.

 500 SeaWorld Dr.

 619/222-6363;
www.seaworld.org

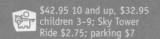 $42.95 10 and up, $32.95
children 3–9; Sky Tower
Ride $2.75; parking $7

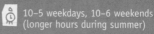 10–5 weekdays, 10–6 weekends
(longer hours during summer)

 2 and up

California Touch Pool, where they can get their hands on starfish and other tide-pool creatures. Also take them to the Shipwreck Café—not only to eat, but also for the impromptu wildlife presentations. Kids will be able to walk right up to otters, penguins, and other creatures for a better look.

The biggest draw for all ages is the Shamu Adventure, starring a troop of trained killer whales. On busy days, you'll need to get to the stadium early and wait up to half an hour (at least!) before the show starts—so be sure the kids are fed and watered beforehand, and bring along some books and toys to keep them busy. Alternatively, the rest of the park quiets down during the Shamu showings, so if you want to forsake the whales altogether, it's a good time to visit the other popular attractions—like the rides and the sharks—as you'll avoid a (sea) lion's share of the crowding.

KEEP IN MIND When the kids start whining—and when you all start dragging—it's a blessing to be able to head over to Shamu's Happy Harbor—a glorified playground, but a playground just the same, where they can climb, jump, dig in sand, slide, and just get wet. Have their bathing suits handy, and then consider shuttling their already-damp selves to the Shipwreck Rapids. The park has lockers if you want to stash dry clothes.

SIMPSON'S GARDEN TOWN NURSERY

Taking a ride into San Diego's backcountry to visit Simpson's plant nursery in Jamul (pronounced "Hah-mool"), about 20 mi from the city's downtown, is like taking a trip back in time. They don't have a telephone, fax machine, or Web site, they don't accept any of those newfangled credit cards, and they don't advertise. And these old-time ways don't seem to hurt them in the least. In fact, they're thriving here, because Simpson's is so beloved by local green thumbs.

Even non-green thumbs enjoy gazing at the plants and flowers, and you will, too. Most of the plants are potted, but arranged in creative ways to mimic jungles, deserts, and other landscapes. This way your attention won't wander as you all wander through the rows of roses, perennials, annuals, herbs, cacti, and palm trees. The unique setup allows you to actually drive through aisles in much of the planting areas (if you find something you want

KEEP IN MIND While in the area, don't miss the Water Conservation Garden (12122 Cuyamaca College Dr. W, 619/660–0614) about 6 mi away in nearby El Cajon. It's an excellent chance for the kids to see how a garden is put together, from the ground up. Plus, there's a lot of whimsy here—like 12-ft-tall pencils, shears, and sprinkler heads (designating design, maintenance, and irrigation areas), animal-shape topiaries, and a "water surprise" where you'll get a little wet. Admission is free.

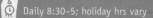
13925 Hwy. 94, Jamul

Free

Daily 8:30–5; holiday hrs vary

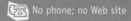
No phone; no Web site

All ages

to buy, you can just load it into your car). You can also head up the hill and visit with the resident pig, Homer Simpson, and other barnyard animals, including a llama, chickens, goats, and a miniature donkey named Matthew. Complementing the quaintness on these 25 acres are some 50 antique automobiles, a wooden windmill, and Burma Shave signs. Also worth exploring is a "museum"—a small building filled with memorabilia devoted to original owner Hal Simpson.

The nursery is now owned and operated by Hal Simpson's granddaughter Cathy and her husband, Lee Smith, but a good old Simpson tradition still endures: when you stop by the office to check out with your plant purchases, you'll be treated to a free, cold, juicy apple to snack on.

EATS FOR KIDS Choose your favorite pie at the nearby **Fillipi's Pizza Grotto** (619/669–1080) or go to **El Campo Mexican Restaurant** (619/669–1662), both at 13881 Campo Road in Jamul. There are also picnic areas at Simpson's if you'd like to eat alfresco.

HEY, KIDS! Way back in the olden days, before portable game consoles and DVD players, about all there was to do during a long car ride was look out the window. Burma Shave and other companies took advantage of this by placing ad signs along the highways—but they put only one line on each sign, so you had to keep reading them for miles to get the whole story. Luckily, Simpson's has placed them a little closer together here, so you'll have to ride only a few yards to read the entire message.

SOLID ROCK GYM

9

If your brood tends to start climbing the walls after too much time cooped up inside, then this place was made for them: the large warehouse-like space is packed with rock-climbing walls studded with colorful footholds and handholds. It's sort of like a mountain brought indoors, and this is nice because your mountaineers can't climb out of your sight—they have to stop at the ceiling (about two stories high).

Climbers of all experience levels flock here to learn and hone their techniques. And getting up the walls is pretty cinchy and safe even for your youngest enthusiasts, as everyone must wear a harness attached to a top-rope belay (rope-securing) station above them, which is in turn counterweighted by a partner in a harness on the ground who controls the slack on the rope. Consequently, a climber can fall only as far as the rope lets him (usually a few inches). Kids under 8 must have a guardian as a belay partner.

HEY, KIDS!

There are many different types of climbing. Climbing up real mountains is called mountaineering. Rock climbing is done over rocky, steep terrain. And ice climbing is done on glaciers and frozen waterfalls.

EATS FOR KIDS

While you're in the area, try a Mexican food mecca, **El Indio Restaurant** (3695 India St., 619/299–0333), beloved by locals and tourists for its famous chips and combination plates. One block north you'll find another local treasure, **Saffron** (3731 India St., 619/574–7737). This is actually two Thai restaurants in one, **Saffron Chicken** and **Saffron Noodles and Sate,** both with tables and take-out. Walk another half block north for dessert at **Gelato Vero Café** for Italian-style ice cream and pastries.

 2074 Hancock St.

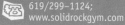 619/299-1124;
www.solidrockgym.com

 $15 M–F; weekends and holidays $19 ages 17 and up, $17 children 4–16; gear rental and lesson fees vary

 M–F 11–10, Sa 9–9, Su 11–7

 4 and up

There are 30 belay stations here to choose from, plus the handholds and footholds are changed often by the staff, so no one gets bored with having to climb the same routes over and over again. Besides the muscle-building workout they'll get from the climbs, your kids will be building their problem-solving skills, flexibility, and balance.

A bonus to coming here is the chance to watch the expert climbers as they traverse the lead cave area in the center area of the building. Watch the wonder on the kids' faces when they see these climbers practically crawl up the walls, then move onto the overhang area where they seem to defy gravity and climb around the inside curve of the wall that arches up overhead—just like Spider-Man.

KEEP IN MIND You can join the gym on a monthly or annual basis if you live in the area, but even if you're just visiting, you can sign up for a lesson, a good deal that includes a day pass and equipment rental. The best lesson for beginners is aptly named Climbing 101.

STUDIO MAUREEN

8

The folks at Studio Maureen love making, showing, and selling art, and they prove it by exhibiting the work of local artists and craftspeople, and by offering an impressive variety of classes where you and your kids can create your own masterpieces.

In the afternoon, Thursday through Saturday, you can drop in at the studio to paint ceramics (note that weekdays tend to be a little quieter). Or, you can sign up for a workshop—most are only a couple of hours long and focus on a specific technique or project. Just call ahead for subjects, times, and fees, and to reserve a space. The beginning ceramics class teaches such basic techniques as hand building, pinch, coil, and slab construction. Other sessions allow you to work in mosaic to create pots and garden stepping-stones, or mold Fimo (polymer clay) to make beads and decorate objects. You can also learn to make paper and then decorate it with marbleizing techniques. At holiday time, special workshops focus on ornament and holiday gift making.

HEY, KIDS! There are almost as many names for craftspeople as there are materials to craft, so here's a rundown on who does what: Potters and ceramicists work with clay. Fiber and textile artists create with fabric or paper materials. Metalsmiths, silversmiths, and goldsmiths work with common and precious metals, as do jewelers and jewelry artists, who also use gemstones and beads. Glassblowers and glass artists work with molten glass. And enamelists decorate the surface of metal pieces with small amounts of molten glass.

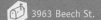

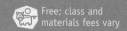
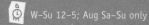

Part of the fun of taking the classes here is that there's a good chance that your teacher will be one of the artists who exhibits work in the studio's adjoining space, the Next Door Gallery. Shows change here about every six weeks. The studio has items for sale, too, that might include pottery, folk art from around the world, handmade jewelry, and clothing. So your browsing isn't too impaired by distractions, the studio keeps sidewalk chalk, markers, and paper on hand for young doodlers.

Speaking of hands, the studio provides two nifty ways to preserve your child's handprint; have them make an impression in a clay heart, or brand a colorful handprint onto a plate. Footprints and other mementos are available, too. Just call ahead for more details and to reserve a time.

EATS FOR KIDS
Nearby is a San Diego landmark; the **Big Kitchen** (3003 Grape St., 619/234-5789) has been serving the community for decades. Try the breakfast burritos or blueberry pancakes. For a quick snack, try **Santos** (3001 Beech St., 619/236-8622) for pastries and drinks.

GETTING THERE It can be a little tricky to find this part of Golden Hill. Traveling on I-5 south (from downtown or farther north) take I-94 east to the 28th Street exit, go right on 28th, then right on Beech. From I-805 north or south, take I-94 west and follow the same directions from the 28th Street exit. But if you are traveling north on I-5 (from the south bay area), you'll take the Pershing Street exit, make a right on 26th Street, go left on A Street, go left on 28th Street, and head right on Beech Street.

SUMMERS PAST FARMS

7

Do you believe in fairies? They sure do at Summers Past Farms, which tries to lure them to the gardens by growing some of their favorite herbs, such as thyme and rosemary. The farm also holds a special fairy festival each June, where you can attend a fairy tea and create wee gardens to try to entice the fairy folk from their hiding spots. With such inducements, even Tinkerbell would be likely to attend.

Principally an herb and flower farm, this is a magical place for humans to visit, too. Not your fancy, fussily manicured kind of landscape, this secret garden incarnate is sweet, wild, and innocent, a living delight with lovely little paths for wandering. Color and fragrance will pleasurably bombard you at every turn as you encounter the Provence-style lavender fields, climb over Monet-like arched bridges, and navigate through a sweet-pea maze (in spring). Herbs might include marjoram, bay leaves, and mint; you can purchase some of

EATS FOR KIDS The espresso cart here serves muffins and juice (on the weekends only). Consider driving a few more miles into the mountain town of Alpine, and try the fried chicken and specialty breads (such as apple nut) at the **Bread Basket Restaurant and Bakery** (1347 Tavern Rd., 619/445–0706).

KEEP IN MIND Like the Fairy Festival, there are other special events here throughout the year. Come to Lavender Day in June to learn how to grow and use it to make soaps, potpourri, and even cookies. Geranium Day in July and Sweet Pea Day in April each include expert tips on these varieties. On Pumpkin Patch Day in October, they break out the hay bales and bring in a special petting zoo for the kids. And there is a special Mother's Day Weekend Brunch and Herb Festival each May (reservations required). Each event includes the option of a pre-reserved, catered picnic lunch.

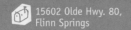 15602 Olde Hwy. 80,
Flinn Springs

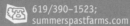 619/390-1523;
summerspastfarms.com

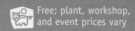 Free; plant, workshop,
and event prices vary

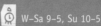 W–Sa 9–5, Su 10–5

 2 and up

them as well as bulbs and flowers inside the property's big red timber barn, a shop with a garden and decorative items.

Let your preschoolers play in the children's garden and explore its little playhouse and tepee, and have them visit with the resident rabbits, kept in cages and fed from garden clippings. You'll also encounter friendly cats and dogs, decidedly uncaged. If you're here the day of a workshop, consider taking one with your older children if they're old enough to appreciate and handle the materials. Together, learn the delicate art of wreath making, drying floral bouquets, soap making, and, of course, gardening.

It is a 25-mi drive east here from downtown San Diego, but the trip's reward is an enchanting afternoon spent wandering the paths, relishing the floral displays, and savoring the scents.

HEY, KIDS! Have you ever seen a fairy? It's hard to catch a glimpse of one because they are quite shy. But according to legend, you can lure them into your garden by growing some of their favorite plants, like they have here. Fairies reportedly like lavender, pansies, bluebells, cosmos, lilacs, and fox-glove. Water fountains, fishponds, and anything that glitters also attracts them. Most important, they don't like ill tempers or bad manners, so it's important that you're in good spirits and well behaved—while you're here, and, well, for the rest of your life—if you hope to see one.

THOMAS WHALEY HOUSE MUSEUM

In the oldest part of the city, there are bound to be a few ghost stories—and that's the case with California Landmark #65 in Old Town San Diego State Historic Park. Not only is it the oldest brick building in Southern California, but it's also an official "haunted house" (designated so by the U.S. Dept. of Commerce) notorious for its supernatural visitors.

Some believe spirits haunt the place because Thomas Whaley built his house in 1857 on the site of the town's gallows, where many people were publicly hanged. The Whaley family also experienced tragedies while they lived here, including the death of children and a suicide. Over the years, visitors to the house have reported strange experiences that they attribute to ghostly presences, including footsteps, voices, music, laughter, scents (cigar smoke and perfume), and even apparitions that disappear into thin air. Whether or not any of this is true, you can bet that kids age 8 and up will want to go on a tour and look for "signs."

HEY, KIDS! In Mexico, *Dia de los Muertos* (Day of the Dead) is an important time when families and friends remember deceased loved ones in a unique celebration. From November 1 to 2, they visit cemeteries to decorate graves with flowers, candles, and other festive items. In their homes, they create altars to their loved one with photographs and objects the person enjoyed in life, such as their favorite food and drink. You can see examples of these traditions in Old Town between October 29 and November 2. There are also graveyard decorations at El Campo Santo and altars at Bazaar del Mundo (see #56).

2482 San Diego Ave.

 $5 ages 13 and up, $3 children 3–12

Daily 10–4:30; F–Sa 10–7 in summer

619/297–7511

 7 and up

As you walk through the house, watch the rocking chairs, which have often been reported to sway on their own (especially the one in the upstairs nursery). In the kitchen, hanging objects sometimes swing by themselves. Listen especially for heavy footsteps (with no one around to make them!); they are supposed to belong to Yankee Jim Robinson, who was hanged on the spot that now houses the archway between the music room and the parlor.

If your group is still hungry for spooky stuff, walk a few blocks southeast to El Campo Santo, a tiny mid-1800s cemetery where late-night hauntings have been reported. Other bets for possible ghost sightings include downtown's Horton Grand Hotel, the *Star of India* sailing ship at the San Diego Maritime Museum (*see #20*), the Point Loma Lighthouse (*see #53*), and the Hotel Del Coronado (*see #47*). And if you've had enough of the paranormal, keep kicking around in the state park (*see #30*).

EATS FOR KIDS Across the street is the **Old Town Mexican Café**—adored by San Diegans and visitors (2489 San Diego Ave., 619/297–4330). Or try **Coyote Café y Cantina** (2461 San Diego Ave., 619/291–4695), another good Mexican spot that also serves grilled-cheese sandwiches and cheeseburgers.

KEEP IN MIND According to child development experts, kids ages 2–6 are particularly vulnerable to fears of monsters and ghosts. If going inside the Whaley House sounds too spooky for your little ones, you can just view it from the outside and walk around back to check out the lovely garden. If your child talks about being afraid, experts suggest that you briefly acknowledge the fear, calmly reassure them, and then distract them by changing the subject or beginning a new activity.

TORREY PINES STATE RESERVE

Those poor dinosaurs. They didn't survive the Ice Age, but luckily, *Pinus Toreyana* did. Better known as the Torrey Pine, this ancient tree's ancestors grow in only two places in the whole world, and you and your family can see most of them here (the rest are on Santa Rosa Island near Santa Barbara). They're easy to recognize—they have gnarled trunks and very long pine needles (8 to 10 inches). Only a few thousand are left, and this preserve was created to protect them.

Many young kids couldn't be less interested in the rarity of the trees, but they will enjoy walking along the sandy hiking trails here. Guided nature walks leave the visitor center on weekends and holidays at 10 and 2, and you can also pick up trail and wildlife guides there if you're striking out on your own. There are six trails ranging from 100 ft to 1.3 mi, but

EATS FOR KIDS Stop for seafood and seasoned fries on the patio at **Nugent's Seafood Grille** (2282 Carmel Valley Rd., Del Mar, 858/792–6100) or fill up on the rolled tacos with guacamole, and other Mexican goodies, at **Roberto's** (2206 Carmel Valley Rd., 858/755–1629).

KEEP IN MIND Looking at the beautiful Pacific Ocean might inspire the kids to go for a swim. If you don't want to hike down the beach trail, just hop in the car and head back down the hill to where you entered the preserve and you'll find Torrey Pines State Beach. From here, you can get to the surf just across the narrow patch of sand. Since you can't eat at the preserve, this is a great place to stop for a picnic, either at the tables near the parking lot, or on a blanket on the beach.

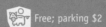

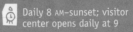

your preschoolers won't need to go farther than the rocks at Red Butte on the Razor Point Trail. They'll like climbing up and down the rugged area (but watch for the steep drop-off on the east side) and exploring the path on the southeast side of the butte that is covered in a canopy of trees and shrubs (it's just their size; adults will have to stoop to get through).

School-age kids can handle most of the trails, but bring along drinking water (it's the only food or drink allowed in the preserve) for the hike. Older kids can take the more challenging, steep, ¾-mi beach trail down to Flat Rock Beach for an up-close look at the water. Every trail has spectacular views of the ocean, so be sure to take a break every now and then and see if you can spot bottlenose dolphins. In the winter, this is a great place to watch for migrating gray whales.

HEY, KIDS! Along with the Torrey Pine, there are some other rare trees that are native to California. The world's tallest tree is the redwood that lives along the central and northern coast. The tallest one towers 368 ft. In the Sierra Nevada Mountains you'll find giant sequoias, known as the largest living organisms, second in height only to the redwood, and they are wider (up to 25 ft in diameter). The oldest known tree is the bristlecone pine, in the east-central part of the state. Some of these trees are 4,600 years old!

VIEJAS OUTLET CENTER

4

Most outlet centers are not intriguing places to take the kids, but then this is not your run-of-the-mill outlet center. Rather, it resembles a stylized Native American village, with pueblo-like buildings, large rock formations, lush native plants, realistic representations of local wildlife, and water gurgling everywhere, from trickling creeks to two-story tall waterfalls. The kids can also run through an interactive fountain that bounces little geysers of water (just be sure to bring along sneakers or water shoes). On top of all that, a spectacular evening show combines dancing water with lasers, pyrotechnics, and music.

The best part is that this is all free, regardless of whether you drop a dime at any of the shops or at the casino just across the street.

The center is owned by the Viejas Band of the Kumeyaay Indians on their reservation land 35 mi east of downtown San Diego. The outdoor venue is filled with architecture,

EATS FOR KIDS Ringing the Center Show Court is a food court; grab a slice of pizza at **Filippi's Pizza Grotto** or a fish taco at **Rubio's Baja Grille.** Sit inside, or take food outdoors to the tables, chairs, and benches throughout the center, or to Viejas Park for a picnic on the grass. Across the street at the Viejas Casino, the **Harvest Buffet** (5000 Willows Rd., 619/445–5400) is open daily for lunch and dinner with salads, pastas, and carving stations.

landscaping, and design details that reflect the Kumeyaay's respect for the natural world, with emphasis on local wildlife, native plants, and imagery important to their culture. The center has meandering paths with surprises around every corner for the kids to discover, like mountain lion tracks and giant pictographs. The 225,000 sq ft complex is entirely stroller friendly and is anchored by two large open areas: Viejas Park, a large circular grass-filled area sprinkled with boulders suitable for climbing, and the Center Show Court, where you'll find the interactive fountain and pyrotechnic shows. A nice reward, especially for the grown-ups, is that no matter where you are in the center, the air is filled with the perpetual stress-busting sounds of bubbling water, calls of local animals, flute music, and sacred chanting.

HEY, KIDS! Check out the structure above the Center Show Court—it's a gigantic dreamcatcher. Many Native American cultures have traditionally hung the round, web-like dreamcatchers over the beds of sleeping children to trap bad dreams and only allow good ones to float through.

KEEP IN MIND There are 39 bronze animal sculptures throughout the grounds in realistic wildlife settings. It's fun to use them in a game of "I Spy" with the kids. The toddlers can easily spot the "birdie" in a pool of water or the "kitty" resting atop a tree, but school-aged kids can seek out a larger range of animals and read the accompanying educational plaques. See if they can find each of these things: a mountain lion carrying a kitten, a slithering rattlesnake, some battling Desert Big Horn Sheep, and a soaring eagle.

WAVE WATERPARK

As glorious as the beaches are in San Diego County, they won't necessarily deliver a "perfect wave" on demand. Wave Waterpark will. Their Flow Rider machine generates a perpetual 6-ft wave by pumping 30,000 gallons of water per minute, creating the perfect place to practice body surfing before your next foray into the less reliable ocean.

Older kids (8 and up) will especially enjoy this 3-acre water park, especially with the 35-ft water slides and inner tubing down the Rio Loco River, which flows around the center of the park. Preschoolers, normally restricted from water-slide activities, get their own slide here, the Little Dipper, and they can also splash away in the children's water playground, with shallow water and interactive pulleys, levers, pipes, and spray guns. Free life vests are available.

The waterpark is owned by the city of Vista, so the on-site pool is competition-size (with lifeguards on duty) and it's also used off-hours for swimming lessons for infants

EATS FOR KIDS The wave park's concessionaires serve up pizza, hot dogs, subs, and other standards, with such clever kids' meal names as "Totally Tubular" and "Wipe-Out."

KEEP IN MIND Planning to head to the beach later? One of the nice things about the waterpark is that it's always clean—local beaches often have water advisory warnings for swimmers because of contamination from ocean pollution. You can check on water safety at specific beaches by calling the county's Dept. of Environmental Health at 619/338–2073 to hear a recording of beaches currently closed for swimming. If the coast is all clear, you can confidently head west to the beaches nearest to Vista in Carlsbad and Oceanside.

161 Recreation Dr., Vista

 760/940-WAVE;
www.wave-waterpark.com

$11.50 general admission
and spectators, $8.50
under 42 inches

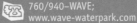

May 25-27 11-5; June 1-Sept 2
10:30-5:30; Sept 3-29 11-5
weekends only

 2 and up

through advanced swimmers, water polo lessons and team practice, and lap swimming in the early morning. Their rescue training programs for kids offer a variety of lifeguarding skills for children ages 7–15, including water safety, first aid, rescue breathing, CPR instruction, and advanced swimming instruction. Also available is an Aqua Camp for third through eighth graders that teaches swimming, water safety, water polo, and other sports. Also watch for special summer events here, such as movies at the park's "Dive-In" Theater.

Although there are lifeguards and employees throughout the park to help keep an eye on your children, bear in mind that parents are expected to supervise the kids at all times and keep them in sight. Bring along your own towels and plenty of sunscreen (and reapply it often).

GETTING THERE Vista is about 40 mi north of downtown San Diego. It makes a good stopping place on a trip up to Orange County or Los Angeles, or as a companion destination if you're visiting the Children's Discovery Museum (*see #49*) or Legoland (*see #36*), both in Carlsbad. To get to Vista from San Diego, take I–5 north about 34 mi, then merge east onto CA–78 (toward Escondido). Take the Vista Village exit, turn left onto Vista Village Drive, and then go right onto Recreation Drive.

WIZARDS OF THE COAST

Pokemon, Dragon Ball Z, Yu-Gi-Oh? It may be Greek to you (actually, it's Japanese), but it's music to kids' ears to hear the names of the trading cards they covet and the games they play. You might have played gin rummy and traded baseball cards, but today card games involve role playing, fierce battles, fantasy worlds, and supernatural creatures. But some things haven't changed. The bones of these games still involve sitting across the table from an opponent with cards between you, and blissfully, there isn't one thing electronic or computerized about that.

Kids come here in swarms to participate in league play with their favorite cards—it's kind of like a bridge tournament for the 21st century. Many different trading card game leagues play here, and there are specified days and times for play of each type of game (just call for details)—and drop-ins are welcome. Even if your kids aren't interested in playing, it's worth a stop here to watch the action—and maybe pick up a few tips. Although it's

KEEP IN MIND If your kids like this stuff, they'll love the Comic-Con International that comes to San Diego's Convention Center for four days each summer. More than just comic books, it's a giant popular arts bonanza with panel discussions, movie screenings, and celebrity appearances. There is also a gigantic vendor area with prime collectible shopping for cards, toys, memorabilia, and comic books. Best of all, the kids will walk out with tons of free stuff—posters, promo cards, buttons, autographed items, and more. Remember the camera so you can snap their picture with Spider-Man or Spawn (619/491-2475, www.comic-con.org).

 1650 Camino Del Rio N #163,
Mission Valley Shopping Center

 619/683-9490;
www.wizards.com

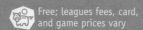 Free; leagues fees, card,
and game prices vary

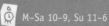 M–Sa 10–9, Su 11–6

 4 and up

not an official activity, a lot of card trading goes on here, too; kids whip out their three-ring binders to display their prized cards and negotiate trades with a savvy that would put most CEOs to shame. Many other types of games are also played here, such as role-playing and miniature games (like Dungeons & Dragons, Star Wars, HeroClix, and 40k Knights).

The spacious game room in the back is filled with tables and chairs, and kids can come back here anytime to play an old-fashioned board game, such as chess, Risk, and Scrabble, for free. If they need a digital fix, they can rent time on video games systems to play PC, Nintendo, and Playstation favorites. The front of the place is a retail shop, filled with the cards (how convenient) and a tremendous collection of board games (even some that you might recognize and want to play).

EATS FOR KIDS

Right across the way in this shopping mall is **Ruby's Diner** (1640 Camino Del Rio N, 619/ 294–7829), with '50s-style diner food such as burgers, hot dogs, and macaroni and cheese. There are also many fast food–type places sprinkled around the mall, such as **Burger King, Mrs. Fields Cookies,** and **Dairy Queen.**

HEY, KIDS! What's a CCG? How about a RPG, or D&D? CCG stands for Collectible Card Game—another name for trading-card games like Pokemon. Although people have collected all sorts of cards for decades, collecting cards for game play started only in 1993 with "Magic: The Gathering" created by Richard Garfield of Wizards of the Coast. RPG stands for Role Playing Game, and D&D (Dungeons & Dragons) is probably the most well known of these, where players assume the roles of characters in an imaginary world; some are played with miniature figures (like HeroClix).

YELLOW BOOK ROAD

It's thrilling to see a group of kids who are excitedly waiting to see one of their heroes, and it's even more gratifying when you find out they're not waiting to meet a sports star or music idol, but a book author such as Janell Cannon (*Stellaluna*) or David Shannon (*No, David*). Your kids will get the chance to do this regularly at Yellow Book Road, an educationally based independent bookstore in the heart of La Mesa Village that hosts authors several times a month.

The 5,000-sq-ft store has many brightly decorated areas for kids to explore, with books and materials to suit every age, from babies through high-schoolers. Former teachers own and run the place, so they are savvy on trends in reading and can recommend books that are both enjoyable and educational. They'll also supply you with lists of recent award winners to guide you in your browsing.

EATS FOR KIDS Enjoy **Por Favor's** Mexican food on their patio (8302 La Mesa Blvd., 619/698–5950). At **Super China Buffet** (7984 La Mesa Blvd., 619/337–6888) there are more than 120 items. Or, try the sandwiches and wraps at **Trolley Stop Café** (8150 La Mesa Blvd., 619/697–3354).

KEEP IN MIND Summer story times often have themes, such as "picnics" or "Christmas in July" that 3- to 7-year-olds can enjoy on Thursday mornings at 10:30. After your literary adventures, you can all explore the rest of La Mesa Village on foot, or hop in the car and head for one of La Mesa's parks. Aztec Park (Aztec Dr. at Morocco Dr.) has a playground and a hillside of grass to roll down. Immense Harry Griffen Park's (9550 Milden St.) 53 acres offer many play areas, with a sandbox, climbing structures, swings, and sports fields. At Jackson Park (Jackson Dr. at Laird), the kids can play safely in the fenced-in playground.

 8315 La Mesa Blvd., La Mesa

 Free

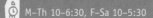 M–Th 10–6:30, F–Sa 10–5:30

619/463–4900;
www.yellowbookroad.com

 All ages

You'll find a good mix of resources for both parents and educators here. In addition to children's literature, the store carries an extensive collection of educational materials that are sought by teachers (you're free to buy them, too, and their inventory is meticulously up-to-date), and the owners even encourage school classes to attend the author visits.

The store publishes a biannual newsletter (available in the store, by mail, or on their Web site) in which they review books, give previews on upcoming author visits, recommend reading lists, and talk about what's up and coming in children's publishing.

HEY, KIDS! With nearly 5,000 new children's books published every year, there's a lot to celebrate during National Children's Book Week each November and Young People's Poetry Week in April. Aside from reading, the Children's Book Council has some suggestions for how to commemorate these special weeks: dress up like your favorite character, have a poetry festival, hold a story-writing contest, share books among friends, celebrate favorite authors, take field trips to literary landmarks, and turn off the TV for a whole week—and read!

THE CLASSICS

"I'M THINKING OF AN ANIMAL... " With older kids you can play 20 Questions: Have your leader think of an animal, vegetable, or mineral (or, alternatively, a person, place, or thing) and let everybody else try to guess what it is. The correct guesser takes over as leader. If no one figures out the secret within 20 questions, the first person goes again. With younger children, limit the guessing to animals and don't put a ceiling on how many questions can be asked. With rivalrous siblings, just take turns being leader. Make the game's theme things you expect to see at your day's destination.

"I SEE SOMETHING YOU DON'T SEE AND IT IS BLUE." Stuck for a way to get your youngsters to settle down in a museum? Sit them down on a bench in the middle of a room and play this vintage favorite. The leader gives just one clue—the color—and everybody guesses away.

FUN WITH THE ALPHABET

"I'M GOING TO THE GROCERY . . . " The first player begins, "I'm going to the grocery and I'm going to buy . . . " and finishes the sentence with the name of an object, found in grocery stores, that begins with the letter "A". The second player repeats what the first player has said, and adds the name of another item that starts with "B". The third player repeats everything that has been said so far and adds something that begins with "C" and so on through the alphabet. Anyone who skips or misremembers an item is out (or decide up front that you'll give hints to all who need 'em). You can modify the theme depending on where you're going that day, as "I'm going to X and I'm going to see . . . "

"I'M GOING TO ASIA ON AN ANT TO ACT UP." Working their way through the alphabet, players concoct silly sentences stating where they're going, how they're traveling, and what they'll do.

FAMILY ARK Noah had his ark—here's your chance to build your own. It's easy: Just start naming animals and work your way through the alphabet, from antelope to zebra.

WHAT I SEE, FROM A TO Z In this game, kids look for objects in alphabetical order—first something whose name begins with "A," next an item whose name begins with "B," and so on. If you're in the car, have children do their spotting through their own window. Whoever gets to Z first wins. Or have each child play to beat his own time. Try this one as you make your way through zoos and museums, too.

JUMP-START A CONVERSATION

WHAT IF . . . ? Riding in the car and waiting in a restaurant are great times to get to know your youngsters better. Begin with imaginative questions to prime the pump.

- If you were the tallest man on earth, what would your life be like? The shortest?
- If you had a magic carpet, where would you go? Why? What would you do there?
- If your parents gave you three wishes, what would they be?
- If you were elected president, what changes would you make?
- What animal would you like to be and what would your life be like?
- What's a friend? Who are your best friends? What do you like to do together?
- Describe a day in your life 10 years from now.

DRUTHERS How do your kids really feel about things? Just ask. "Would you rather eat worms or hamburgers? Hamburgers or candy?" Choose serious and silly topics—and have fun!

FAKER, FAKER Reveal three facts about yourself. The catch: One of the facts is a fake. Have your kids ferret out the fiction. Take turns being the faker. Fakers who stump everyone win.

KEEP A STRAIGHT FACE

"HA!" Work your way around the car. First person says "Ha." Second person says "Ha, ha." Third person says "Ha" three times. And so on. Just try to keep a straight face. Or substitute "Here, kitty, kitty, kitty!"

WIGGLE & GIGGLE Give your kids a chance to stick out their tongues at you. Start by making a face, then have the next person imitate you and add a gesture of his own—snapping fingers, winking, clapping, sneezing, or the like. The next person mimics the first two and adds a third gesture, and so on.

JUNIOR OPERA During a designated period of time, have your kids sing everything they want to say.

IGPAY ATINLAY Proclaim the next 30 minutes Pig Latin time, and everybody has to talk in this fun code. To speak it, move the first consonant of every word to the end of the word and add "ay." "Pig" becomes "igpay," and "Latin" becomes "atinlay." To words that being with a vowel, just add "ay" as a suffix.

MORE GOOD TIMES

BUILD A STORY "Once upon a time there lived . . . " Finish the sentence and ask the rest of your family, one at a time, to add another sentence or two. Bring a tape recorder along to record the narrative—and you can enjoy your creation again and again.

NOT THE GOOFY GAME Have one child name a category. (Some ideas: first names, last names, animals, countries, friends, feelings, foods, hot or cold things, clothing.) Then take turns naming things that fall into that category. You're out if you name something that doesn't belong in the category—or if you can't think of another item to name. When only one person remains, start again. Choose categories depending on where you're going or where you've been—historic topics if you've seen a historic sight, animal topics before or after the zoo, upside-down things if you've been to the circus, and so on. Make the game harder by choosing category items in A-B-C order.

COLOR OF THE DAY Choose a color at the beginning of your outing and have your kids be on the lookout for things that are that color, calling out what they've seen when they spot it. If you want to keep score, keep a running list or use a pen to mark points on your kids' hands for every item they spot.

CLICK If Cam Jansen, the heroine of a popular series of early reader books, says "Click" as she looks at something, she can remember every detail of what she sees, like a camera (that's how she got her nickname). Say "Click!" Then give each one of your kids a full minute to study a page of a magazine. After everyone has had a turn, go around the car naming items from the page. Players who can't name an item or who make a mistake are out.

THE QUIET GAME Need a good giggle—or a moment of calm to figure out your route? The driver sets a time limit and everybody must be silent. The last person to make a sound wins.

high fives

FAVORITE FIVE
Balboa Park
Bazaar del Mundo
La Jolla Shores
San Diego Wild Animal Park
San Diego Zoo

OUTDOORS
Mission Bay

CULTURAL ACTIVITY
Old Town San Diego State Historic Park

MUSEUM
Reuben H. Fleet Science Center

WACKY
San Diego Model Railroad Museum

NEW & NOTEWORTHY
Knott's Soak City U.S.A.

SOMETHING FOR EVERYONE

HISTORICAL

ON THE WILD SIDE

PARKS AND GARDENS

PERFECT PICNIC PLACES

PLANES, TRAINS, AND AUTOS

RAINY DAYS

SCIENTIFIC TERRIFIC

SHOW TIME

TIRE THEM OUT

TOURS

WATER, WATER EVERYWHERE

WAY UP HIGH

ALL AROUND TOWN

OLD TOWN
Basic Brown Bear Factory **57**
Bazaar Del Mundo **56**
Old Town San Diego State Historic Park **30**
Solid Rock Gym **9**
Thomas Whaley House Museum **6**

POINT LOMA
Cabrillo National Monument **53**

SANTEE
Lake Murray **37**
Santee Drive-In **13**

VISTA
Wave Waterpark **3**

MANY THANKS

I owe a great debt of gratitude to Paul Eisenberg, my editor at Fodor's, for his clear vision and compassionate spirit; to Claire Yezbak Fadden, Sharon and Larry Bay and their crew at *San Diego Family Magazine,* who treat their writers with respect and caring; and to Annie Ross, a great researcher and translator and even better friend, for sharing her expertise.

Thanks must also go to my parents, Spencer and Yolonda Cuadra, for their amazing insight to raise their family in San Diego, and for their unending support (and to my sisters, Linda, Laura, and Carri, for theirs, too!); Joyce and Bill Winters, for bringing up their six kids here, too (including my husband, Tom) and for all their help; my dear friend Lynn Holmes Leavitt, with whom I shared so many great adventures while growing up in San Diego and with whom I continue to get in trouble today—only now we get to take our own kids along for the fun; my playgroup buddies, with whom I explored many of the destinations in this book while we toted along all our infants, toddlers, strollers, and diaper bags—and laughed every step of the way; and to just about everybody in the Eastlake/Olympic View community who shared great ideas and graciously invited my kids over to play while I wrote—thank you! My deep appreciation goes out to my incredible, amazing, funny, and kind-hearted children, Calen, Katie, and Will, who inspire me constantly. Of all the treasures I've found around San Diego, they are certainly the most precious of all. And most of all, my love and gratitude to my husband, Tom, whose patience, humor, faith, and support (and great pep talks) help me every single day, and without whom this book could not have been written.

—Cynthia Cuadra Winters